PACIFIC BASIN BOOKS

Editor: Kaori O'Connor

JAPAN
MADAME CHRYSANTHEMUM

BY PIERRE LOTI

Translated by Laura Ensor

KPI

LONDON, BOSTON, SYDNEY AND HENLEY

First published in 1920
This edition published in 1985 by KPI Limited
14 Leicester Square, London WC2H 7PH, England,

Distributed by
Routledge & Kegan Paul plc
14 Leicester Square, London WC2H 7PH, England,

Routledge & Kegan Paul Inc
9 Park Street, Boston, Mass., 02108, USA,

Routledge & Kegan Paul
c/o Methuen Law Book Company
44 Waterloo Road
North Ryde, NSW 2113, Australia and

Routledge & Kegan Paul plc
Broadway House, Newtown Road,
Henley-on-Thames, Oxon RG9 1EN, England

Printed in Great Britain by
St Edmundsbury Press, Bury St Edmunds, Suffolk

ISBN 0-7103-0138-3

INTRODUCTION
TO THIS EDITION

TRAVELLERS OF all kinds who turn towards Japan today can have no better guide than the writer Pierre Loti, whose book *Madame Chrysanthemum*[1] – the first Western romance to be set in Japan – was part of the vogue for all things Japanese that swept Western art, music and literature in the late nineteenth century, and inspired Puccini's opera *Madame Butterfly*.

Loti's prose has often been compared to poetry, for it is wonderfully subtle and suggestive, hauntingly evocative of a world as fragile as a painted teacup. Loti's is a romantic *milieu* of lantern processions, teahouse parties, paper parasols and silken kimono sleeves. But although Loti's treatment is delicate it is not superficial, and for all their prettiness the lanterns do not keep the shadows at bay.

Madame Chrysanthemum is an autobiographical novel, a true account of the temporary marriage of a French lieutenant and his geisha in the 1880's, when Japan was becoming Westernized. It is a love story but not a conventional one, for the officer who wrote under the name Pierre Loti was in love, not with his Westernized geisha, but with the old Japan that he saw slipping away into modernism. *Madame Chrysanthemum* is a compelling portrait of a vanished age, but above all it is a sensitive account of the bittersweet meeting of East and West in Japan, a century ago.

Julien Marie Viaud, whom the world came to know as Pierre Loti, was born in the tideway port of Rochefort in western

France on January 14, 1850. Theodore Viaud, a provincial civil servant, played little part in his son's upbringing, and the boy grew up in an adoring female circle consisting of his mother Nadine, an aunt, two grandmothers, a great aunt and a sister nineteen years older than himself, who smothered the child with overprotective affection. Julien's childhood was isolated and oppressively intimate by turns, for his female relations discouraged contact with other children and kept him at home with tutors until he was ten. Within the Viaud household the days passed with a monotonous uneventfulness enlivened only by the rich inner life that young Julien pursued from his earliest years, a life in which fantasy and imagination were given the free rein denied him in other spheres.

The colonies became the focus of the boy's reveries, an interest that was encouraged by his brother Gustave, older by twelve years, who was a naval surgeon in the colonial service. The letters and curios that Gustave sent back from his posting in Tahiti made Julien yearn for an adventurous life in the colourful and romantic lands that lay *ailleurs outre mer* – somewhere beyond the seas – far from the black skirts and grey skies of Rochefort. By the age of thirteen the boy had decided to follow his brother into the navy, a plan that had to be abandoned when Gustave died on the way home from a tour of duty in Indonesia. Julien blamed it on the imperialistic policies of the day which sent the finest men of France abroad to die in dreadful conditions for colonial gains, and this was the beginning of the anti-colonial theme that would recur in the works of Pierre Loti.

Nadine Viaud refused to lose her only remaining son to the navy, and it took another family tragedy to free Julien to pursue his chosen career. When Julien was seventeen his father was imprisoned on charges of embezzlement, and although Theodore Viaud was later cleared of all charges, the family was still obliged to pay back the missing monies. A naval career, subsidised by the state if the candidate could pass the examinations, offered the only chance for Julien to assume the burden of family support. He duly attained the standard required for

entrance to the naval college at Brest, and although his upbringing had ill prepared him for the rigorous life of a naval cadet, he
applied himself to learning the ropes with ruthless determina-
tion. After receiving his commission in 1870, he embarked on a
series of voyages that would, in the course of forty-two years of
active service, carry him to North and West Africa, Turkey, the
South Pacific, Japan, Tonkin and China.

Of all those who have sailed under the flag of France, few can
have been as strange and exotic as Lieutenant Viaud. The child
who had been kept at home against his will became an adult
whose appetite for travel and adventure could never be satisfied.
The boy who had been yoked to petty provincial moralities grew
up to lead a defiantly unconventional life. The young Julien
whose upbringing had been so repressive became Pierre Loti –
the man of passion.

When he finally reached the foreign lands he had dreamed of,
he was not content to regard them serenely from the bridge of his
ship. Whenever possible he would slip away to immerse himself
in the culture of the place, wearing their clothes, living their life,
learning their language and loving their women. In Tahiti he
shared an island idyll with a pretty Polynesian who gave him the
love-name '*loti*'. He dallied with a creole in Senegal and in
Turkey he assumed the name of Arik Ussum and contrived an
affair with a Circassian *khadine* from a harem. Yet for all this he
remained a consummately capable officer who won the acceptance and admiration of his men and his superiors. On the many
occasions when men under his command encountered him
ashore pursuing his double life, it was understood that they
". . . should not appear to recognize him were their paths to
cross, and this was scrupulously observed."[2]

The affairs of Lieutenant Viaud were faithfully recorded in the
journals he had kept from childhood. After the much-regretted
end of his Turkish *amour* he wrote a full *memoire* of the romance in
an effort to recapture some of his lost happiness, and this account
formed the basis of his first book *Aziyadé*, which appeared in
1877. The modest success of this first effort led his publishers to

request a second book, an offer that was very welcome as he had to support himself and the family in Rochefort on the slender salary of a lieutenant. *Rarahu*, based on his Tahitian adventures, was received with choruses of acclaim and by 1881 when he published *Le Roman d'un Spahi*, based on his Senegalese interlude, his reputation as a brilliant writer was firmly established. 'Pierre Loti', as Julien Viaud was now known outside the Service, was feted in all the literary circles and given the entrée to the finest salons in Europe, but the man who was perfectly at home in ship's cabin or kasbah could never feel at ease in Society. Although he could now well afford to buy his way out of the Service, he preferred to carry on with his naval career.

In the summer of 1885, when he had newly arrived in Japan for a tour of duty at Nagasaki, Loti wrote a short and startling letter to his friend Mme Juliette Adam, co-founder of the *Nouvelle Revue*:

> "Last week I was married . . . to a young girl of seventeen. She is called Okane-san. We celebrated with a lantern procession and a tea party. The validity of the marriage is entirely at the whim of the two parties."[3]

Loti's was an arrangement that had become common in large Japanese ports like Nagasaki and Yokohama, where officers of foreign navies were allowed to contract 'marriages' with young Japanese women or '*musumes*', both sides accepting that the liaison was a temporary one. For his part, the man would undertake to establish the girl in an apartment, provide her with a servant, visit her when he chose to do so and pay for her attentions on a monthly basis. For her part, the girl was expected to provide her protector with all the comforts of a married man. Having entered into this custom of the country, Loti – the arch-romantic – could find no pleasure in his 'marriage'. The very heartlessness of the arrangement chilled him, and he was further saddened by the effect of Western influences on the Japanese. To Loti, the clash of the two cultures was symbolized by the ungainly sight of Japanese men dressed in kimonos and bowler hats, and by the mercenary behaviour of the odious go-between Kangorou. Throughout *Madame Chrysanthemum*, Loti returns to another of his recurrent themes – in the meeting of East and West, it is always the East who is ultimately the loser.

Western curiosity about the people and culture of Japan had been growing steadily since 1853, when Japan opened her doors to the west after more than two centuries of self-imposed isolation. By the 1870's, travel books on Japan had appeared in every major European language, but although Loti was not the first writer to deal with Japan, he was the first novelist to do so, and the distinction is a crucial one. Because of the enormous popular success it enjoyed on publication, *Madame Chrysanthemum* reached a much larger public than the travel books or the specialist studies of Japanese art that were popular in intellectual circles, and there can be no doubt that it was Loti's romantic vision of life in Japan that most influenced the public of the day. Among those who came under the spell of *Madame Chrysanthemum* was the painter Vincent Van Gogh. It was his favourite book, and led him to make a study of Japanese *ukiyo-e* prints that contributed much to the development of his mature painting style.[4]

In 1898, five years after the publication of *Madame Chrysanthemum*, a story set in Japan and entitled *Madam Butterfly* appeared in the American *Century Magazine*. The author of the piece, an American lawyer called John Luther Long, had never been to Japan, and although he maintained that it was based on an authentic episode, much of his story was patently derived from Loti's novel. In Long's version the girl Ki-kou san becomes Cho-cho san; her servant Oyouki becomes maid Suzuki and the unpleasant Kangorou becomes Goro. Although Prince Yamadori, Consul Sharples and the arrogant Lieutenant Pinkerton are entirely Long's creations, the story is largely Loti's. Long's story was turned into a play, and the play in turn provided the starting point for Puccini's opera.[5] Puccini originally intended to turn the play into a one-act opera. When he later decided to write an opera of the full three-act length, the librettists returned to Loti's

Madame Chrysanthemum for many of the scenes and details that are central to the final version of *Madame Butterfly*, which premiered at La Scala, Milan in 1904.

Pierre Loti, Commander Julien Viaud, retired from the French navy in 1910. Although his writing had brought him world fame, great wealth, and many honours including election to the *Academie Française*, the distinctions he prized most highly were those he had earned in naval service. He died at Hendaye, in the Basque country, on June 10, 1923.

In *Madame Chrysanthemum*, Pierre Loti writes:

"Some day, when man shall have made all things alike, the earth will be a dull, tedious dwelling place, and we shall have to give up travelling and seeking for a change that shall no longer be found."[6]

If that day should come, Loti's work ensures that what has been lost will never be forgotten. Until then, his life inspires the belief that romance is still to be sought and found *ailleurs outre mer* – somewhere beyond the seas.

KAORI O'CONNOR

NOTES

1 *Madame Chrysanthemum* was first published in France by Calmann-Lévy in 1893, under the title *Madame Chrysanthème*. In this edition, the French spelling is retained throughout the text.

2 Blanch, Lesley, *Pierre Loti: Portrait of an Escapist*. Collins, London, 1983: p 118.

3 In *Lettres de Pierre Loti a Madame Juliette Adam (1880–1922)*. Librairie Plon, Paris, 1924; p 69.

4 Whitford, Frank, *Japanese Prints and Western Painters*. Studio Vista, London, 1977; p 187.

5 The death of Kikou-san/Cho-cho-san/Cio-cio-san does not occur in Loti's story or in Long's. This element was added by the playright David Belasco, who adapted the magazine story *Madame Butterfly* for the stage. See Carner, Mosco, *Puccini: A Critical Biography*, Gerald Duckworth & Co, London, 1958; p 120.

6 Loti, Pierre, *Japan: Madame Chrysanthemum*, KPI, London, 1985; p 16.

JAPAN

TO MADAME
LA DUCHESSE DE RICHELIEU.

Madame la Duchesse,

Allow me to crave your acceptance of the following work, as a respectful tribute of my attachment.

I felt some hesitation in offering it, for its main incident cannot be deemed altogether proper; but I have striven that in its expression at least, it should not sin against good taste, and I trust that my endeavours have been successful.

It is the diary of a summer of my life, in which I have changed nothing, not even the dates, thinking as I do, that in our efforts to arrange *matters we often only succeed in disarranging them. Although the most important role may appear to devolve on Madame Chrysanthème, it is very certain that the three principal personages are* myself, Japan, *and the* effect *produced on me by that country.*

Do you remember a certain photograph—rather ridiculous I must admit—representing that big fellow Yves, a Japanese girl and myself, grouped closely together as we were placed side by side by a Nagasaki artist? You smiled when I assured you that the carefully combed little creature placed between us two, had been one of our neighbours. *Kindly welcome my book with the same indulgent smile, without seeking therein a meaning either good or bad; in the same spirit that you would receive some quaint bit of pottery, some grotesquely carved ivory idol, or some preposterous trifle brought back for you from this singular fatherland of* all preposterousness.

Believe me with the deepest respect,
 Madame la Duchesse,
  Your affectionate

PIERRE LOTI.

INTRODUCTION.

At sea, about two o'clock in the morning, on a clear night, under a star-lit sky.

Yves stood near me on the bridge, and we were talking of the country, so utterly unknown to us both, to which the chances of our destiny were now wafting us. As we were to cast anchor the following day, we enjoyed the state of expectation, and formed a thousand plans.

"As for me," I said, "I shall at once marry."

"Ah!" returned Yves, with the indifferent air of a man whom nothing can surprise.

"Yes—I shall choose a little yellow-skinned woman with black hair and cat's eyes. She must be pretty. Not much bigger than a doll. You shall have a room in our house. A little paper house, in the midst of green gardens, prettily shaded. We shall live among flowers, everything around us shall blossom, and each morning our dwelling shall be filled with nosegays, nosegays such as you have never dreamt of.

Yves now began to take an interest in these plans for my future household; indeed, he would have listened with as much confidence, if I had manifested the intention of taking temporary vows in some monastery of this new country, or of marrying some island queen and shutting myself up with her in a house built of jade, in the middle of an enchanted lake.

In reality I had quite made up my mind to carry out the scheme I had unfolded to him. Yes, actually, led on by ennui and solitude, I had gradually arrived at dreaming of and looking forward to this absurd marriage. And then, above all, to live for awhile on land, in some shady nook, amid trees and flowers. How tempting it sounded after the long months we had been wasting at the Pescadores (hot and arid islands, devoid of freshness, woods, or streamlets, full of faint odours of China and of death).

We had made great way in latitude, since our vessel had quitted that Chinese furnace, and the constellations in the sky had undergone a series of rapid changes; the Southern Cross had dis·appeared at the same time as the other austral stars; and the Great Bear rising on the horizon, was almost on as high a level as it is in the French sky. The fresh evening breeze soothed and revived us, bringing back to us the memory of our summer night watches on the coast of Brittany.

What a distance we were, however, from those familiar coasts! What a terrible distance!

i.

Aᴛ dawn of day we sighted Japan.

Precisely at the foretold moment Japan arose before us, afar off, like a clear and distinct dot in the vast sea, which for so many days had been but a blank space.

At first we saw nothing in the rising sun but a series of tiny pink-tipped heights (the foremost portion of the Fukai islands). Soon, however, appeared all along the horizon, like a thick cloud, a dark veil over the waters, Japan itself; and little by little out of the dense shadow arose the sharp opaque outlines of the Nagasaki mountains.

The wind was dead against us, and the strong breeze, which steadily increased, seemed as if the country were blowing with all its might against us, in a vain effort to drive us away from its shores. The sea, the rigging, the vessel itself, all vibrated and quivered as if with emotion.

II

By three o'clock in the afternoon all these far-off objects drew close to us, so close, indeed, that they overshadowed us by their rocky masses and dense green thickets.

We now entered into a shady kind of channel enclosed between two high ranges of mountains, curiously symmetrical in shape—like stage scenery, very fine, though unlike nature. It seemed as if Japan opened to our view, through a fairy-like rent, which thus allowed us to penetrate into her very heart.

Nagasaki, as yet unseen, must be at the

extremity of this long and curious bay. All around us was admirably green. The strong sea-breeze had suddenly fallen, and was succeeded by a perfect calm ; the atmosphere, now very warm, was laden with the perfume of flowers. In the valley resounded the ceaseless whirr of the cicalas, answering each other from one shore to another ; the mountains re-echoed with innumerable sounds ; the whole country seemed to vibrate like crystal. On our way we passed among myriads of Japanese junks, gliding softly, wafted by imperceptible breezes on the unruffled water ; their motion could scarcely be heard, and their white sails, stretched out on yards, fell languidly in a thousand horizontal folds like window-blinds, their strangely contorted poops rising up castle-wise in the air, reminding one of the towering ships of the middle ages. In the midst of the intense greenery of this wall of mountains, they stood out with a snowy whiteness.

What a country of verdure and shade is Japan ; what an unlooked-for Eden !

Beyond us, at sea, it must have been full daylight ; but here, in the recesses of the valley, we already felt the impression of evening ; beneath the summits in full sunlight, the base of the mountains and all the thickly wooded parts near the water's edge were steeped in twilight.

The passing junks, gleaming white against the background of dark foliage, were silently and dexterously manœuvred by small yellow men, stark naked, with long hair piled up in womanlike fashion on their heads. Gradually, as we advanced further up the green channel, the perfumes became more penetrating, and the monotonous chirp of the cicalas swelled out like an orchestral crescendo. Above us, on the luminous sky, sharply delineated between the mountains, a species of hawk hovered about, screaming out with a deep human voice, " Han! Han! Han!" its melancholy call lengthened out by the surrounding echoes.

All this fresh and luxurious nature bore the impress of a peculiar Japanese type, which seemed to pervade even the mountain tops, and consisted, as it were, in an untruthful aspect of too much prettiness. The trees were grouped in clusters, with the same pretentious grace as on the lacquered trays. Large rocks sprung up in exaggerated shapes, side by side with rounded lawn-like hillocks; all the incongruous elements of landscape were grouped together as though it were an artificial creation.

Looking intently, here and there might be seen, often built in counterscarp on the very brink of an abyss, some old, tiny, mysterious pagoda, half hidden in the foliage of the overhanging trees; bringing to the minds of new arrivals such as ourselves, the sense of unfamiliarity and strangeness; and the feeling that in this country, the Spirits, the Sylvan Gods, the antique symbols, faithful guardians of the woods and forests, were unknown and uncomprehended.

When Nagasaki rose before us, the sight that greeted our eyes was disappointing; situated at the foot of green overhanging mountains, it looked like any other commonplace town. In front of it lay a tangled mass of vessels, carrying all the flags of the world; steamboats just as in any other port, with dark funnels and black smoke, and behind them quays covered with factories: nothing in fact was wanting in the way of ordinary, trivial, every-day objects.

Some day, when man shall have made all things alike, the earth will be a dull, tedious dwelling-place, and we shall have even to give up travelling and seeking for a change which shall no longer be found.

At about six o'clock, we dropped anchor noisily amid the mass of vessels already there, and were immediately invaded.

Invaded by a mercantile, bustling, comical Japan, which rushed upon us in full boat-loads, full junks, like a rising sea ; little men and little women coming in a continuous, uninterrupted stream, without cries, without squabbles, noiselessly, each one making so smiling a bow that it was impossible to be angry with them, and that indeed by reflex action we smiled and bowed also. They all carried on their backs little baskets, little boxes, receptacles of every shape, fitting into each other in the most ingenious manner, each one containing several others, and multiplying till they filled up everything, in endless number ; from these they drew forth all manners of curious and unexpected things, folding screens, slippers, soap, lanterns, sleeve-links, live cicalas chirping in little cages, jewelry, tame white mice turning little cardboard mills, quaint photographs, hot soups and stews in bowls ready to be served out in rations to the crew ;—china, a legion of vases, teapots, cups, little pots and plates. In one moment, all this was unpacked, spread out with astounding rapidity and a certain talent for arrangement ; each seller squatting monkey-like, hands touching feet, behind his fancy ware —always smiling, bending low with the most

engaging bows. Under the mass of these many-coloured things, the deck presented the appearance of an immense bazaar ; the sailors, very much amused and full of fun, walked among the heaped-up piles, taking the little women by the chin, buying anything and everything, throwing broadcast their white dollars. But, good gracious, how ugly, mean and grotesque all those folk were. Given my projects of marriage, I began to feel singularly uneasy and disenchanted.

Yves and myself were on duty till the next morning, and after the first bustle, which always takes place on board when settling down in harbour—(boats to lower, booms to swing

out, running rigging to make taut)—we had
nothing more to do but to look on. We said
to one another : " Where are we in reality ?

—In the United States ?—In some English
Colony in Australia, or in New Zealand ? "
Consular residences, custom-house offices,
manufactories ; a dry dock in which a Russian
frigate was lying ; on the heights the large
European concession, sprinkled with villas, and

on the quays, American bars for the sailors. Further off, it is true, further off, far away behind these common-place objects, in the very depths of the immense green valley, peered thousands upon thousands of tiny black houses, a tangled mass of curious appearance, from which here and there emerged some higher, dark red, painted roofs, probably the true old Japanese Nagasaki which still exists. And in those quarters, who knows, there may be, lurking behind a paper screen, some affected cat's-eyed little woman, whom perhaps in two or three days (having no time to lose) I shall marry!! But no, the picture painted by my fancy has faded. I can no longer see this little creature in my mind's eye; the sellers of the white mice have blurred her image; I fear now, lest she should be like them.

At nightfall, the decks were suddenly cleared as by enchantment; in a second, they had all shut up their boxes, folded their sliding screens, their trick fans, and, humbly bowing to each of us, the little men and little women have disappeared.

Slowly, as the shades of night closed around us mingling all things in the bluish darkness, this Japan surrounding us, became once more, by degrees, little by little, a fairy-like and enchanted country. The great mountains, now all black, were mirrored and doubled in the still water at their feet on which we floated, reflecting therein their sharply reversed outlines, and presenting the mirage of fearful precipices, over which we hung:—the stars also were reversed in their order, making, in the depths of the imaginary abyss, a sprinkling of tiny phosphorescent lights.

Then all Nagasaki became profusely illuminated, covering itself with multitudes of lanterns: the smallest suburb, the smallest village was lit up; the tiniest hut perched up on high among the trees, and which in the daytime was invisible, threw out its little glow-worm glimmer. Soon there were numberless lights all over the country, on all the shores of the bay, from top to bottom of the mountains; myriads of glowing fires shone out in the darkness, conveying the impression of a vast capital, rising up around us in one bewildering amphitheatre. Beneath, in the silent waters, another town, also illuminated, seemed to descend into the depths of the abyss. The night was balmy, pure, delicious; the atmosphere laden with the perfume of flowers came wafted to us from the mountains. From the "tea houses" and other nocturnal resorts, the sound of guitars reached our ears, seeming in the distance the sweetest of music. And the whirr of the cicalas—which, in Japan, is one of the continuous noises of life, and which in a few days we shall no longer even be aware of, so completely is it the background and foundation of all the other terrestrial sounds — was sonorous, incessant, softly monotonous, just like the cascade of a crystal waterfall.

III.

THE next day the rain came down in torrents, a regular downpour, merciless and unceasing, blinding and drenching everything,— a thick rain so dense that it was impossible to see through it from one end of the vessel to the other. It seemed as though the clouds of the whole world had amassed themselves in Nagasaki bay, and had chosen this great green funnel to stream down to their hearts' content. And it rained, it rained, it became almost as dark as night, so thickly did the rain fall. Through a

veil of crumbled water, we still perceived the
base of the mountains, but the summits were
lost to sight among the great sombre masses
weighing down upon us. Above us shreds of
clouds, seemingly torn from the dark vault.
draggled across the trees, like vast grey rags,—
continually melting away in water, torrents of
water. There was wind too, and it howled
through the ravines with a deep-sounding tone.
The whole surface of the bay, bespattered by
the rain, flogged by the gusts of wind that blew
from all quarters, splashed, moaned and seethed
in violent agitation.

What wretched weather for a first landing,
and how was I to find a wife through such a
deluge, in an unknown country !

No matter ! I dressed myself and said to
Yves, who smiled at my obstinate determina-
tion in spite of unfavourable circumstances :
" Hail me a ' sampan,' brother, please."
Yves then, by a motion of his arm through
the wind and rain, summoned a kind of little
white wooden sarcophagus which was skipping
near us on the waves, sculled by a couple of
yellow boys stark naked in the rain. The craft
approached us, I jumped into it, then through a
little trap-door shaped like a rat-trap that one

of the scullers throws open for me, I slipped in and stretched myself at full length on a mat in what is called the " cabin " of a sampan.

There was just room enough for my body to lie in this floating coffin, which is moreover scrupulously clean, white with the whiteness of new deal boards. I was well sheltered from the rain, that fell pattering on my lid, and thus I started off for the town, lying in this box, flat on my stomach, rocked by one wave, roughly shaken by another, at moments almost over-turned ; and through the half-opened door of my rat-trap I saw, upside down, the two little creatures to whom I had entrusted my fate, children of eight or ten years of age at the most, who, with little monkeyish faces, had however fully developed muscles like miniature men, and were already as skilful as any regular old salts.

They began to shout ; no doubt we were approaching the landing-place. And indeed, through my trap-door, which I had now thrown wide open, I saw quite near to me the grey flag-stones on the quays. I got out of my sarcophagus and prepared to set foot for the first time in my life on Japanese soil.

All was streaming around us, and the irritating, tiresome rain dashed into my eyes.

No sooner had I landed, than there bounded
towards me about a dozen strange beings, of
what description it was almost impossible to make

out through the blinding showers—a species
of human hedge-hog, each dragging some large
black thing; they came screaming around me

and stopped my progress. One of them opened and held over my head an enormous closely-ribbed umbrella, decorated on its transparent surface with paintings of storks; and they all smiled at me in an engaging manner with an air of expectation.

I had been forewarned: these were only the *djins* who were touting for the honour of my preference; nevertheless I was startled at this sudden attack, this Japanese welcome on a first visit to land (the *djins* or *djin-richisans*, are the runners who drag little carts, and are paid for conveying people to and fro, being hired by the hour or the distance, as cabs are with us).

Their legs were naked; to-day they were

very wet, and their heads were hidden under
large shady conical hats.   By way of water-
proofs they wore nothing less than mats of
straw, with all the ends of the straws turned
outwards bristling like porcupines ; they seemed
clothed in a thatched roof.   They went on
smiling, awaiting my choice.

Not having the honour of being acquainted
with any of them in particular, I choose at haphazard the djin with the umbrella and get into
his little cart, of which he carefully lowers the
hood.   He draws an oil-cloth apron over my
knees, pulling it up to my face, and then advancing near, asks me in Japanese something which
must have meant : " Where to, sir ? "   To
which I reply in the same language, " To the
Garden of Flowers, my friend."

I said this in the three words I had parrot-
like learnt by heart, astonished that such sounds
could mean anything, astonished too at their
being understood.   We started off, he running at
full speed, I dragged along by him, jerked about
in his light chariot, wrapped in oiled cloth, shut
up as if in a box ;—both of us unceasingly
drenched all the while, and dashing all around
us the water and mud of the sodden ground.

" To the *Garden of Flowers*," I had said, like
an habitual frequenter of the place, and quite

surprised at hearing myself speak. But I was less ignorant about Japan than might have been supposed. Many of my friends had, on their return home from that country, told me about it, and I knew a great deal; the *Garden of Flowers* is a *tea-house*, an elegant rendezvous. There, I would inquire for a certain Kangourou-San, who is at the same time interpreter, washerman, and confidential agent for the intercourse of races. Perhaps this very evening, if all went well, I should be introduced to the bride destined to me by mysterious fate. This thought kept my mind on the alert during the panting journey we have been making, the djin and myself, one dragging the other, under the merciless downpour.

Oh, what a curious Japan I saw that day, through the gaping of my oil-cloth coverings! from under the dripping hood of my little cart! A sullen, muddy, half-drowned Japan. All these houses, men or beasts, hitherto only known to me by drawings; all these, that I had beheld painted on blue or pink backgrounds of fans or vases, now appeared to me in their hard reality, under a dark sky, with umbrellas and wooden shoes, with tucked-up skirts and pitiful aspect.

At moments the rain fell so heavily that I

tightly closed up every chink and crevice, and the noise and shaking benumbed me, so that I completely forgot in what country I was. In the hood of the cart were holes, through which little streams ran down my back. Then, re-membering that I was going for the first time in my life through the very heart of Nagasaki, I

cast an inquiring look outside, at the risk of receiving a douche : we were trotting along through a mean, narrow little back street (there are thousands like it, a perfect labyrinth of them) the rain falling in cascades from the tops of the roofs on the gleaming flagstones below, rendering everything indistinct and vague through the misty atmo-sphere. At times we passed by a lady, strug-gling with her skirts, unsteadily tripping along in her high wooden shoes, looking exactly like the figures painted on screens, tucked up under a gaudily daubed paper umbrella. Or else we passed a pagoda, where an old granite monster, squatting in the water, seemed to make a hideous, ferocious grimace at me.

How immense this Nagasaki is! Here had
we been running hard for the last hour, and still
it seemed never-ending. It is a flat plain, and
one could never suppose from the offing that so

vast a plain could lie in the recesses of this
valley.

It would, however, have been impossible for
me to say where I was, or in what direction we
had run; I abandoned my fate to my djin and
to my good luck.

What a steam-engine of a man my djin was! I had been accustomed to the Chinese runners, but they were nothing by the side of this fellow. When I part my oil-cloths to peep at anything, he is naturally always the first object in my foreground : his two naked, brown muscular legs, scampering one after the other, splashing all around, and his bristling hedgehog back bending low in the rain. Do the passers-by, gazing at this little dripping cart, guess that it contains a suitor in quest of a bride ?

At last my vehicle stops, and my djin, with many smiles and precautions lest any fresh rivers should stream down my back, lowers the hood of the cart ; there is a break in the storm, and the rain has ceased. I had not yet seen his face ; by exception to the general rule, he is good-looking ;—a young man of about thirty years of age, of intelligent and strong appearance, and an open countenance. Who could have foreseen that a few days later this very djin.— But no, I will not anticipate, and run the risk of throwing beforehand any discredit on Chrysanthème.

We had therefore reached our destination, and found ourselves at the foot of a tall over-hanging mountain ; probably beyond the limits of the town, in some suburban district. It apparently became necessary to continue our journey on foot, and climb up an almost perpendicular narrow path. Around us, a number of small country houses, garden walls, and high bamboo palisades closed in the view. The green hill crushed us with its towering height; the heavy, dark clouds lowering over our heads seemed like a leaden canopy confining us in this unknown spot; it really seemed as though the complete absence of perspective inclined one all the better to notice the details of this tiny corner, muddy and wet, of homely Japan, now lying before our eyes. The earth was very red. The grasses and wild flowers bordering the pathway were strange to me;—nevertheless, the palings were covered with convolvuli like our own, and I recognised in the gardens, china asters, zinnias, and other familiar flowers. The atmosphere seemed laden with a curiously complicated odour, something besides the perfume of the plants and soil, arising no doubt from the human dwelling-places,— a mingled smell, I fancied, of dried fish and incense. Not a creature was to be seen; of the inhabitants, of their homes and life, there was not a vestige, and I might have imagined myself anywhere in the world.

My djin had fastened up his little cart under
a tree, and together we clambered the steep
path on the slippery red soil.

"We are going to the *Garden of Flowers*,
are we not?" I inquired, anxious to ascertain
if I had been under-
stood.

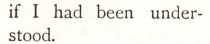

"Yes, yes," replied
the djin, "it is up there,
and quite near."

The road turned,
steep banks hemming it
in and darkening it. On
one side, it skirted the
mountain all covered
with a tangle of wet
ferns; on the other ap-
peared a large wooden
house almost devoid of
apertures and of evil aspect ; it was there that
my djin halted.

What, that sinister-looking house was the
Garden of Flowers? He assured me that it
was, and seemed very sure of the fact. We
knocked at a big door which opened immediately,
slipping back in its groove. Then two funny
little women appeared, oldish-looking, but with
evident pretensions to youth : exact types of

the figures painted on vases, with their baby
hands and feet.

On catching sight of me, they threw themselves on all fours, their faces touching the
floor. Good gracious! what can be the matter?
Nothing at all, it is only the ceremonious salute

to which I am as yet unaccustomed. They rise,
and proceed to take off my boots (one never
keeps on one's shoes in a Japanese house),
wiping the bottom of my trousers and feeling
my shoulders to see if I am wet.

What always strikes one on first entering a
Japanese dwelling is the extreme cleanliness,
the white and chilling bareness of the rooms.

Over the most irreproachable mattings, without a crease, a line, or a stain, I am led upstairs to
the first storey and ushered into a big empty room,
absolutely empty ! The paper walls are mounted
on sliding panels, which fitting into each other,
can be made to disappear entirely,—and all one
side of the apartment opens like a verandah on
to the green country and the grey sky beyond.
By way of a chair, I am given a square piece of
black velvet, and behold me seated low, in the
middle of this large empty room, which by its
very vastness is almost chilly. The two little
women (who are the servants of the house and
my very humble servants too), await my orders,
in attitudes expressive of the profoundest
humility.

It seemed extraordinary that the quaint
words, the curious phrases I had learnt during
our exile at the Pescadores Islands—by sheer
dint of dictionary and grammar book, without
attaching the least sense to them—should mean
anything. But so it seemed, however, for I
was at once understood.

I wish in the first place to speak to one
M. Kangourou, who is interpreter, washerman,
and matrimonial agent. Nothing could be

better : they know him and will go at once in search of him ; and the elder of the waiting-maids gets ready for the purpose her wooden clogs and her paper umbrella.

Next I demand a well-served repast, composed of the greatest delicacies of Japan. Better and better, they rush to the kitchen to order it.

Finally, I beg they will give tea and rice to my djin, who is waiting for me below ;—I wish, in short, I wish many things, my dear little dollies, which I will mention by degrees and with due deliberation, when I shall have had time to assemble the necessary words. But, the more I look at you the more uneasy I feel as to what my *fiancée* of to-morrow may be like. Almost pretty, I grant you, you are,—in virtue of quaintness, delicate hands, miniature feet, but ugly after all, and absurdly small. You look like ouistitis, like little china ornaments, like I don't know what. I begin to understand that I have arrived at this house at an ill-chosen moment. Something is going on which does not concern me, and I feel that I am in the way.

From the beginning I might have guessed as much, notwithstanding the excessive politeness of my welcome ; for I remember now, that

while they were taking off my boots downstairs, I heard a murmuring chatter overhead.
then a noise of panels moved quickly along
their grooves, evidently to hide from me something I was not intended to see; they were
improvising for me the apartment in which I
now am—just as in menageries they make a
separate compartment for some beasts when the
public is admitted.

Now I am left alone while my orders are
being executed, and I listen attentively,
squatted like a Buddha on my black velvet
cushion, in the midst of the whiteness of the
walls and mats.

Behind the paper partitions, worn-out voices,
seemingly numerous, are talking in low tones.
Then rises the sound of a guitar, and the song
of a woman, plaintive and gentle in the echoing
sonority of the bare house, in the melancholy
of the rainy weather.

What one can see through the wide-open
verandah is very pretty, I will admit; it
resembles the landscape of a fairy tale.   There
are admirably wooded mountains, climbing
high into the dark and gloomy sky, and hiding
in it the peaks of their summits, and, perched
up among the clouds—a temple.   The atmosphere has that absolute transparency, the

distance that clearness which follows a great downpour of rain; but a thick pall, still heavy with moisture, remains suspended over all, and on the foliage of the hanging woods still float great flakes of grey fluff, which remain there, motionless. In the foreground, in front of and below all this almost fantastic landscape, is a miniature garden where two beautiful white cats are taking the air, amusing themselves by pursuing each other through the paths of a Lilliputian labyrinth, shaking from their paws the sand, which is still wet. The garden is as conventional as possible : not a flower, but little rocks, little lakes, dwarf trees cut in a grotesque fashion; all this is not natural, but it is most ingeniously arranged, so green, so full of fresh mosses !

In the rain-soaked country below me, to the very furthest end of the vast scene, reigns a great silence, an absolute calm. But the woman's voice, behind the paper wall, continues to sing in a key of gentle sadness, and the accompanying guitar has sombre and even gloomy notes.

Stay though ! Now the music is somewhat quicker—one might even suppose they were dancing !

So much the worse ! I shall try to look

between the fragile divisions, through a crack which has revealed itself to my notice.

What a singular spectacle it is ; evidently the gilded youth of Nagasaki holding a great clandestine orgy! In an apartment as bare as my own, there are a dozen of  them, seated in a circle on the ground, attired in long blue cotton dresses with pagoda sleeves, long, sleek and greasy hair surmounted by European pot hats ; and beneath these, yellow, worn out, bloodless, foolish faces On the floor are a number of little spirit-lamps, little pipes, little lacquer trays, little tea-pots, little cups—all the accessories and all the remains of a Japanese feast, resembling nothing so much as a doll's tea-party. In the midst of this circle of dandies are three over-dressed women, one might say three weird visions, robed in garments of pale and undefinable colours, embroidered with golden monsters; and their great chignons arranged with fantastic art, stuck full of pins and flowers. Two are seated and turn their back to me : one is holding the guitar, the other singing with that soft and pretty voice ; —thus seen furtively, from behind, their pose, their hair, the nape of the neck, all is exquisite,

and I tremble lest a movement should reveal to me faces which might destroy the enchantment.   The third one is on her feet, dancing before this areopagus of idiots, with their lanky locks and pot hats.   What a shock when she turns round !   She wears over her face the horribly grinning, deathly mask of a spectre or vampire. The mask unfastened, falls. And behold ! a darling little fairy of about twelve or fifteen years of age, slim, and already a coquette, already a woman,—dressed in a long robe of shaded dark blue china crape, covered with embroidery representing bats—grey bats, black bats, golden bats.

Suddenly there are steps on the stairs, the light footsteps of barefooted women pattering over the white mats. No doubt the first course of my lunch just about to be served. I quickly fall back, fixed and motionless, upon my black velvet cushion. There are three of them now, three waiting-maids who arrive in single file, with smiles and curtsies. One offers me the spirit-lamp and the tea-pot, another preserved fruits in delightful little plates, the third, absolutely indefinable objects upon gems of little trays. And they grovel before me on the floor, placing all this plaything of a meal at my feet.

At this moment, my impressions of Japan are charming enough ; I feel myself fairly launched upon this tiny, artificial, fictitious world, which I felt I knew already from the paintings of lacquer and porcelains. It is so exact a representation ! The three little squatting women, graceful and dainty, with their narrow slits of eyes, their magnificent chignons in huge bows, smooth and shining as boot-polish, and the little tea-service on the floor, the landscape seen through the verandah, the pagoda perched among the clouds ; and over all the same affectation everywhere, in every detail. Even the woman's melancholy voice, still to be heard behind the paper partition, was so evidently the way they should sing, these musicians I had so often seen painted in amazing colours on rice-paper, half closing their dreamy eyes in the midst of impossibly large flowers. Long before I came to it, I had perfectly pictured this Japan to myself. Nevertheless in the reality it almost seems to be smaller, more finicking than I had imagined it, and also much more mournful, no doubt by reason of that great pall of black clouds hanging over us and this incessant rain.

While awaiting M. Kangourou (who is dressing himself it appears, and will be here shortly), it may be as well to begin lunch.

In the daintiest bowl imaginable, adorned with flights of storks, is the most wildly impossible soup made of sea-weed. After which there are little fish dried in sugar, crabs in sugar, beans in sugar, and fruits in vinegar and pepper. All this is atrocious, but above all unexpected and unimaginable. The little women make me eat, laughing much, with that perpetual irritating laugh, which is the laugh peculiar to Japan,—they make me eat, according to their fashion, with dainty chop-sticks, fingered with mannered grace. I am becoming accustomed to their faces. The whole effect is refined,—a refinement so utterly different from our own, that at first sight I understand nothing of it, although in the long-run it may end by pleasing me.

Suddenly there enters, like a night butterfly awakened in broad daylight, like a rare and surprising moth, the dancing-girl from the other compartment, the child who wore the horrible mask. No doubt she wishes to have a look at me. She rolls her eyes like a timid kitten, and then all at once tamed, nestles against me, with a coaxing air of childishness, which is a delightfully transparent assumption. She is slim, elegant, delicate, and smells sweet; drolly painted, white as plaster, with a little circle of rouge marked very precisely in the middle of each cheek, the mouth reddened, and a touch of gilding outlining the under lip. As they could not whiten the back of the neck on account of all the delicate little curls of hair growing there, they had, in their love of exactitude, stopped the white plaster in a straight line, which might have been cut with a knife, and in consequence at the nape appears  a square of natural skin of a deep yellow.

An imperious note sounds on the guitar, evidently a summons! Crac! Away she goes, the little fairy, to rejoice the drivelling fools on the other side of the screens.

Supposing I marry this one, without seeking any further. I should respect her as a child committed to my care; I should take her for what she is: a fantastic and charming play-thing. What an amusing little household I should set up! Really short of marrying a china ornament, I should find it difficult to choose better.

At this moment enters M. Kangourou, clad in a suit of grey tweed, which might have come from *La Belle Jardinière* or the *Pont Neuf*, with a pot hat and white thread gloves. His countenance is at once foolish and cunning; he has hardly a nose, hardly any eyes. He makes a real Japanese salutation: an abrupt dip, the hands placed flat on the knees, the body making a right angle to the legs, as if the fellow were breaking in two; a little snake-like hissing (produced by sucking the saliva between the teeth, and which is the expression *nec plus ultra* of obsequious politeness in this country).

"You speak French, M. Kangourou?"

"Yes, sir" (renewed bows).

He makes one for each word I utter, as if he were a mechanical toy pulled by a string; when he is seated before me on the ground, he limits himself to a duck of the head—always accom-panied by the same hissing noise of the saliva.

"A cup of tea, M. Kangourou?"

Fresh salute and an extra affected gesticulation with the hands, as if to say, "I should hardly dare. It is too great a condescension on your part. However, anything to oblige you."

He guesses at the first words what I require from him.

"Of course," he replies, "we will see about it at once; in a week's time, as it happens, a family from Simonosaki, in which there are two charming daughters, will be here."

"What! in a week! You don't know me, M. Kangourou! No, no, either now, to-morrow, or not at all."

Again a hissing bow, and Kangourou-San catching my agitation, begins to pass in feverish review, all the young persons at his disposal in Nagasaki.

"Let us see—there was Mdlle. Œillet. What a pity that I had not spoken a few days sooner! So pretty! So clever at playing the guitar. It is an irreparable misfortune; she was engaged only yesterday by a Russian officer."

"Ah! Mdlle. Abricot!—Would she suit me, Mdlle. Abricot? She is the daughter of a wealthy China merchant in the Decima Bazaar, a person of the highest merit; but she would be very dear: her parents, who think a great deal

of her, will not let her go under a hundred yen *
a month.   She is very accomplished, thoroughly
understands commercial writing, and has at her
finger ends more than two thousand characters
of learned writing.   In a poetical competition
she gained the first prize with a sonnet composed in praise of '*the blossoms of the black-
thorn hedges seen in the dew of early morning.*'
Only, she is not very pretty : one of her eyes is
smaller than the other, and she has a hole in her
cheek, resulting from an illness of her childhood."

"Oh no ! on no account that one !   Let us
seek amongst a less distinguished class of young
persons, but without scars.   And how about
those on the other side of the screen, in those
fine gold-embroidered dresses ?   For instance,
the dancer with the spectre mask, M.
Kangourou ? or again she who sings in so
dulcet a strain and has such a charming
nape to her neck ? "

He does not, at first, understand my drift ;
then when he gathers my meaning, he shakes
his head almost in a joking way, and says :

" No, sir, no ! Those are only *Guéchas*,† sir—
Guéchas ! "

" Well, but why not a *Guécha ?*   What odds
can it be to me, whether they are *Guéchas* or

---

* A yen is equal to four shillings.
† *Guéchas* are professional dancers and singers trained at the Yeddo
Conservatory.

not ? " Later on, no doubt, when I understand
Japanese affairs better, I shall appreciate myself
the enormity of my proposal : one would really
suppose I had talked of marrying the devil.

At this point M. Kangourou suddenly calls to
mind one Mdlle. Jasmin. Heavens! how was
it he did not think of her at once ; she is absolutely and exactly what I want ; he will go to-
morrow or this very evening, to make the
necessary overtures to the parents of this young
person who live a long way off, on the opposite
hill, in the suburb of Diou-djen-dji. She is a
very pretty girl of about fifteen. She can probably be engaged for about eighteen or twenty
dollars a month, on condition of presenting her
with a few dresses of the best fashion, and of
lodging her in a pleasant and well-situated
house,—all of which a man of gallantry like
myself could not fail to do.

Well, let us fix upon Mdlle. Jasmin then,
—and now we must part ; time presses. M.
Kangourou will come on board to-morrow to
communicate to me the result of his first pro-
ceedings and to arrange with me for the inter-
view. For the present he refuses to accept any
remuneration ; but I am to give him my washing,
and to procure him the custom of my brother
officers of the *Triomphante*. It is all settled.
Profound bows,—they put on my boots again at

the door. My djin, profiting by the interpreter kind fortune has placed in his way, begs to be recommended to me for future custom; his stand is on the quay; his number is 415, inscribed in French characters on the lantern of his vehicle (we have a number 415 on board, one Le Goëlec, gunner, who serves the left of one of my guns; happy thought, I shall remember this); his price is sixpence the journey, or five pence an hour, for his customers. Capital; he shall have my custom, that is promised. And now, let us be off. The waiting-maids, who have escorted me to the door, fall on all fours as a final salute, and remain prostrate on the threshold—as long as I am still in sight down the dark pathway, where the rain trickles off the great over-arching bracken upon my head.

IV

THREE days have passed. Night is closing, in an apartment which has been mine since yesterday. Yves and I, on the first floor, move restlessly over the white mats, striding up and down the great bare room, of which the thin, dry flooring cracks beneath our footsteps ; we are both of us rather irritated by prolonged expectation. Yves, whose impatience shows itself the most freely, from time to time takes a look out of the window. As for myself, a chill suddenly seizes me, at the idea that I have chosen, and purpose to inhabit this lonely house, lost in the midst of the suburb of a totally strange town, perched high on the mountain and almost opening upon the woods.

What wild notion can have taken possession of me, to settle myself in surroundings so utterly foreign and unknown, breathing of isolation and sadness ?   The waiting unnerves me, and I beguile the time by examining all the little details of the building.   The woodwork of the ceiling is complicated and ingenious.   On the partitions of white paper which form the walls, are scattered tiny, microscopic, blue-feathered tortoises.

" They are late," said Yves, who is still looking out into the street.

As to being late, that they certainly are, by a good hour already, and night is falling, and the boat which should take us back to dine on board will be gone.   Probably we shall have to sup, Japanese fashion to-night, heaven only knows where.   The people of this country have no sense of punctuality, or of the value of time.

Therefore I continue to inspect the minute and comical details of my dwelling.   Here, instead of handles such as we should have put to pull these movable partitions, they have made little oval holes, just the shape of a finger-end, and into which one is evidently to put one's thumb.   These little holes have a bronze orna-

mentation, and on looking closely, one sees that
the bronze is curiously chased: here is a lady
fanning herself; there, in the next hole, is repre-
sented a branch of cherry in full blossom.
What eccentricity there is in the taste of this
people! To bestow assiduous labour on such
miniature work, and then to hide it at the bottom
of a hole to put one's finger in, looking like a
mere spot in the middle of a great white panel;
to accumulate so much patient and delicate
workmanship on almost imperceptible accessories, and all to produce an effect which is
absolutely *nil*, an effect of the most utter bareness and nudity.

Yves still continues to gaze forth, like Sister
Anne. From the side on which he leans, my
verandah overlooks a street, or rather a road
bordered with houses, which climbs higher and
higher, and loses itself almost immediately in
the verdure of the mountain, in the fields of tea,
the underwood and the cemeteries. As for
myself, this delay finishes by irritating me for
good and all, and I turn my glances to the
opposite side: the other front of my house, also
a verandah, opens first of all upon a garden;
then upon a marvellous panorama of woods and
mountains, with all the venerable Japanese
quarters of Nagasaki lying confusedly like a black
ant-heap, six hundred feet below us. This even-

ing, in a dull twilight, notwithstanding that it is a twilight of July, these things are melancholy. There are great clouds heavy with rain and showers, ready to fall, travelling across the sky. No, I cannot feel at home, in this strange dwelling I have chosen; I feel sensations of extreme solitude and strangeness; the mere prospect of passing the night in it gives me a shudder of horror.

"Ah! at last, brother," said Yves, "I believe, —yes, I really believe she is coming at last."

I look over his shoulder, and I see—a back view of a little doll the finishing touches to whose toilette are being put in the solitary street; a last maternal glance given to the enormous bows of the sash, the folds at the waist. Her dress is of pearl-grey silk, her *obi* (sash) of mauve satin; a sprig of silver flowers trembles in her black hair; a parting ray of sunlight touches the little figure; five or six persons accompany her. Yes! it is undoubtedly Mdlle. Jasmin; they are bringing me my *fiancée!*

I rush to the ground floor inhabited by old Madame Prune my landlady, and her aged husband; they are absorbed in prayer before the altar of their ancestors.

"Here they are, Madame Prune," I cry in Japanese; "here they are! Bring at once the tea, the lamp, the embers, the little pipes for the ladies, the little bamboo pots for spittoons! Bring up as quickly as possible all the accessories for my reception!"

I hear the front door open, and hasten upstairs again. Wooden clogs are deposited on the floor, the staircase creaks gently under the little bare feet. Yves and I look at each other, with a longing to laugh.

An old lady enters,—two old ladies,—three old ladies, emerging from the doorway one after another with jerking and mechanical salutations, which we return as best we can, fully conscious of our inferiority in this particular style. Then come persons of intermediate age, —then quite young ones, a dozen at least, friends, neighbours, the whole quarter in fact. And the whole company, on arriving, becomes confusedly engaged in reciprocal salutations : I salute you,—you salute me,—I salute you again, and you return it,—and I re-salute you again, and I express that I shall never, never be able to return it according to your high merit,— and I bang my forehead against the ground, and you stick your nose between the planks of the flooring, and there they are, on all fours one before the other ; it is a polite dispute, all anxious to yield precedence as to sitting down, or passing first, and compliments without end are murmured in low tones, with faces against the floor.

They seat themselves at last, smiling, in a ceremonious circle ; we two remaining standing, our eyes fixed on the staircase. And at length emerges, in due turn, the little aigrette of silver flowers, the ebony chignon, the grey silk robe and mauve sash of Mdlle. Jasmin, my fiancée !

Heavens ! why, I know her already ! Long before setting foot in Japan, I had met with her, on every fan, on every tea-cup—with her silly air, her puffy little visage, her tiny eyes, mere gimlet-holes above those expanses of impossible pink and white which are her cheeks.

She is young, that is all I can say in her favour ; she is even so young that I should almost scruple to accept her. The wish to laugh quits me suddenly, and instead, a profound chill fastens on my heart. What ! share an hour of my life even with that little doll ? Never !

The next question is, how to get out of it ?

She advances smiling, with an air of repressed triumph, and behind her looms M. Kangourou, in his suit of grey tweed. Fresh salutes, and

behold her on all fours, she too, before my landlady and before my neighbours. Yves,

the big Yves, who is not going to be married,
stands behind me, with a comical grimace, hardly
repressing his laughter,—while to give myself
time to collect my ideas, I offer tea in little cups,
little spittoons and embers to the company.

Nevertheless, my discomfited air does not
escape my visitors. M. Kangourou anxiously
inquires :

"How do I like her?" And I reply in a
low voice, but with great resolution :

"Not at all! I won't have that one.
Never!"

I believe that this remark was almost understood in the circle around me. Consternation
was depicted on every face, the jaws dropped,
the pipes went out. And now I address my
reproaches to Kangourou : " Why had he
brought her to me in such pomp, before friends
and neighbours of both sexes, instead of showing her to me discreetly as if by chance, as I
had wished ? What an affront he will compel
me now to put upon all these polite persons !"

The old ladies (the mamma no doubt and
aunts), prick up their ears, and M. Kangourou
translates to them, softening as much as possible, my heartrending decision. I feel really
almost sorry for them ; the fact is, that for
women who, not to put too fine a point upon it,
have come to sell a child, they have an air I
was not prepared for : I can hardly say an air
of *respectability* (a word in use with us, which is
absolutely without meaning in Japan), but an
air of unconscious and good-natured simplicity ;
they are only accomplishing an act perfectly
admissible in their world, and really it all resembles, more than I could have thought
possible, a *bonâ fide* marriage.

" But what fault do I find with the little girl?"
asks M. Kangourou, in consternation.

I endeavour to present the matter in the most flattering light:

"She is very young," I say; "and then she is too white, too much like our own women. I wished for a yellow one just as a change."

" But that is only the paint they have put on her, sir! Beneath it, I assure you, she is yellow."

Yves leans towards me and whispers:

" Look over there, brother, in that corner by the last panel; have you noticed the one who is sitting down ? "

Not I. In my annoyance I had not observed her; she had her back to the light, was dressed in dark colours, and sat in the careless attitude of one who keeps in the background. The fact is this one pleased me much better. Eyes with long lashes, rather narrow, but which would have been called good in any country in the world; almost an expression, almost a thought. A coppery tint on her rounded cheeks; a straight nose; slightly thick lips, but well modelled and with pretty corners. Less young than Mdlle. Jasmin, about eighteen years of age perhaps, already more of a woman. She wore an expression of ennui, also of a little contempt, as if she regretted her attendance at a spectacle which dragged so much, and was so little amusing.

" M. Kangourou, who is that young lady over there, in dark blue ? "

"Over there, sir? A young lady called
Mdlle. Chrysanthème. She came with the
others you see here ; she is only here as a spec-
tator. She pleases you?" said he with eager
suddenness, espying a way out of his difficulty.

Then, forgetting all his politeness, all his cere-
moniousness, all his Japanesery, he takes her by
the hand, forces her to rise, to stand in the
dying daylight, to let herself be seen. And she,

who has followed our eyes and begins to guess
what is on foot, lowers her head in confusion,
with a more decided but more charming pout,
and tries to step back, half sulky, half smiling.

"It makes no difference," continues M.
Kangourou, "it can be arranged just as well
with this one ; she is not married either, sir !"

She is not married! Then why didn't the
idiot propose her to me at once instead of the
other, for whom I have a feeling of the greatest
pity, poor little soul, with her pearl grey dress,
her sprig of flowers, her expression which grows
sadder, and her eyes which twinkle like those of
a child about to cry.

"It can be arranged, sir !" repeats Kangourou again, who at this moment appears to
me a go-between of the lowest type, a rascal of
the meanest kind.

Only, he adds, we, Yves and I, are in the
way during the negotiations. And, while
Mdlle. Chrysanthème remains with her eyelids
lowered, as befits the occasion, while the
various families, on whose countenances may be
read every degree of astonishment, every phase
of expectation, remain seated in a circle on my
white mats, he sends us two into the verandah,
and we gaze down into the depths below us,
upon a misty and vague Nagasaki, a Nagasaki
melting into a blue haze of darkness.

Then ensue long discourses in Japanese, arguments without end. M. Kangourou, who is washerman and low scamp in French only, has returned for these discussions to the long formulas of his country. From time to time I express impatience, I ask this worthy creature whom I am less and less able to consider in a serious light :

"Come now, tell us frankly, Kangourou, are we any nearer coming to some arrangement? is all this ever going to end?"

"In a moment, sir, in a moment;" and he resumes his air of political economist seriously debating social problems.

Well, one must submit to the slowness of this people. And, while the darkness falls like a veil over the Japanese town, I have leisure to reflect, with as much melancholy as I please, upon the bargain that is being concluded behind me.

Night has closed in, deep night; it has been necessary to light the lamps.

It is ten o'clock when all is finally settled, and M. Kangourou comes to tell me :

"All is arranged, sir : her parents will give her up for twenty dollars a month,—the same price as Mdlle. Jasmin."

On hearing this, I am possessed suddenly

with extreme vexation that I should have made up my mind so quickly to link myself in ever so fleeting and transient a manner with this little creature, and dwell with her in this isolated house.

We come back into the room; she is the centre of the circle and seated; and they have placed the aigrette of flowers in her hair. There is actually some expression in her glance, and I am almost persuaded that she— this one—thinks.

Yves is astonished at her modest attitude, at her little timid airs of a young girl on the verge of matrimony; he had imagined nothing like it in such a marriage as this, nor I either, I must confess.

"She is really very pretty, brother," said he; "very pretty, take my word for it!"

These good folks, their customs, this scene, strike him dumb with astonishment; he cannot get over it, and remains in a maze. "Oh! this is too much," and the idea of writing a long letter to his wife at Toulven, describing it all, diverts him greatly.

Chrysanthème and I join hands. Yves too advances and touches the dainty little paw;— after all, if I wed her, it is chiefly his fault; I should never have remarked her without his observation that she was pretty. Who can tell how this strange arrangement will turn out? Is it a woman or a doll? Well, time will show.

The families having lighted their many-coloured lanterns swinging at the ends of slight sticks, prepare to beat a retreat with many compliments, bows and curtsies. When it is a question of descending the stairs, no one is willing to go first, and at a given moment, the whole party are again on all fours, motionless and murmuring polite phrases in under-tones.

"*Haul back there !*" said Yves, laughing and employing a nautical term used when there is a stoppage of any kind.

At length they all melt away, descend the stairs with a last buzzing accompaniment of civilities and polite phrases finished from one step to another in voices which gradually die away. He and I remain alone in the un-friendly empty apartment, where the mats are still littered with the little cups of tea, the absurd little pipes, and the miniature trays.

" Let us watch them go away!" said Yves, leaning out. At the door of the garden is a re-newal of the same salutations and curtsies, and then the two groups of women separate, their bedaubed paper lanterns fade away trembling in the distance, balanced at the extremity of flexible canes which they hold in their finger-tips, as one would hold a fishing-rod in the dark to catch night-birds. The procession of the unfortunate Mdlle. Jasmin mounts upwards towards the mountain, while that of Mdlle.

Chrysanthème winds downwards by a narrow old street, half stairway, half goat-path, which leads to the town.

Then we also depart. The night is fresh,

silent, exquisite, the eternal song of the cicalas fills the air. We can still see the red lanterns of my new family, dwindling away in the distance, as they descend and gradually become lost in that yawning abyss, at the bottom of which lies Nagasaki.

Our way, too, lies downwards, but on an opposite slope by steep paths leading to the sea.

And when I find myself once more on board, when the scene enacted on the hill up above recurs to my mind, it seems to me that my betrothal is a joke, and my new family a set of puppets.

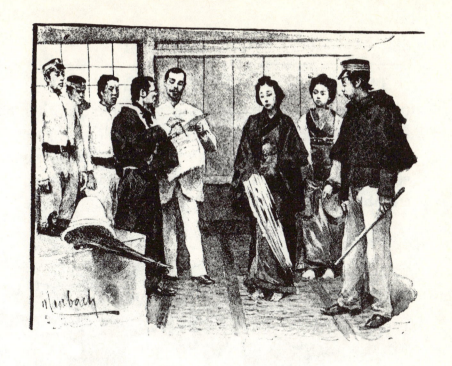

V.

Iᴛ is three days now since my marriage was an accomplished fact.

In the lower part of the town, in the middle of one of the new cosmopolitan districts, in the ugly pretentious building which is a kind of register office, the deed has been signed and countersigned, with marvellous hieroglyphics, in a large book, in the presence of those ridiculous little creatures, formerly silken-robed *Samouraï*, but now called policemen, and dressed up in tight jackets and Russian caps.

The ceremony took place in the full heat of mid-day; Chrysanthème and her mother arrived there together, and I went alone. We seemed to have met for the purpose of ratifying some discreditable contract, and the two women trembled in the presence of these ugly little

individuals, who, in their eyes, were the personification of the law.

In the middle of their official scrawl, they made me write in French my name, Christian name, and profession. Then they gave me an extraordinary document on a sheet of rice-paper, which set forth the permission granted me by the civilian

authorities of the Island of Kiu-Siu, to inhabit
a house situated in the suburb of Diou-djen-dji,
with a person called Chrysanthème, the said

permission being available under protection of
the police, during the whole of my stay in Japan.

In the evening, however, up there in our own
quarter, our little marriage became a very pretty

affair,—a procession carrying lanterns, a festive tea and some music. It was indeed high time.

Now we are almost an old married couple, and we are gently settling down into every-day habits.

Chrysanthème tends the flowers in our bronze vases, dresses herself with studied care, proud of her socks with the divided big toe, and strums all day on a kind of long-necked guitar, producing therefrom plaintive and sad sounds.

VI.

In our home, all has the appearance of a Japanese picture: we have nothing but little folding-screens, little curiously shaped stools bearing vases full of nosegays, and at the further end of the apartment, in a nook forming an altar, a large gilded Buddha sits enthroned in a lotus.

The house is just as I had fancied it should be in the many dreams of Japan I had made before my arrival, during my long night watches: perched on high, in a peaceful suburb, in the

midst of green gardens ;—made up of paper
panels, and taken to pieces according to one's
fancy, like a child's toy. Whole families of
cicalas chirp day and night under our old resounding roof. From our verandah, we have a
bewildering bird's-eye view of Nagasaki, of its
streets, its junks and its great pagodas, which,
at certain hours, is lit up at our feet like some
fairylike scene.

VII.

As a mere outline, little Chrysanthème has been seen everywhere and by everybody. Whoever has looked at one of those paintings on china or on silk that now fill our bazaars, knows by heart the pretty stiff head-dress, the leaning figure, ever ready to try some new gracious salutation, the scarf fastened behind in an enormous bow, the large falling sleeves, the dress slightly clinging about the ankles with a little crooked train like a lizard's tail.

But her face, no, everyone has not seen it ; there is something special about it.

Moreover, the type of women the Japanese paint mostly on their vases is an exceptional one in their country. It is almost exclusively among the nobility that these personages are found with their long pale faces, painted in tender rose-tints, and silly long necks which give them the appearance of storks. This distinguished type (which I am obliged to admit was also Mdlle. Jasmin's) is rare, particularly at Nagasaki.

In the middle class and the people, the ugliness is more pleasant and sometimes becomes a kind of prettiness. The eyes are still too small and hardly able to open, but the faces are rounder, browner, more vivacious; and in the women there remains a certain vagueness in the features, something childlike which prevails to the very end of their lives.

They are so laughing, so merry, all these little Niponese dolls! Rather a forced mirth, it is true, studied and at times with a false ring in it; nevertheless one is attracted by it.

Chrysanthème is an exception, for she is melancholy. What thoughts can be running through that little brain? My knowledge of her language is still too restricted to enable me to find out. Moreover, it is a hundred to one that she has no thoughts whatever. And even if she had, what do I care?

I have chosen her to amuse me, and I would really rather she should have one of those insignificant little thoughtless faces like all the others.

VIII.

WHEN night closes in, we light two hanging lamps of a religious character, which burn till morn, before our gilded idol.

We sleep on the floor, on a thin cotton mattress, which is unfolded and laid out over our white mats. Chrysanthème's pillow is a little wooden block, scooped out to fit exactly the nape of the neck, without disturbing the elaborate head-dress, which must never be taken down ; the pretty black hair I shall probably never see undone. My pillow, a Chinese model, is a kind of little square drum covered over with serpent skin.

We sleep under a gauze mosquito net of

sombre greenish blue, dark as the shades of
night, stretched out on an orange-coloured
ribbon. (These are the traditional colours, and
all the respectable families of Nagasaki possess
a similar gauze.) It envelops us like a tent;
the mosquitoes and the night-moths dance
around it.

    *   *   *   *   *   *   *

This sounds very pretty, and written down
looks very well. In reality, however, it is not
so; something, I know not what, is wanting,
and it is all very paltry. In other lands, in the
delightful isles of Oceania, in the old lifeless
quarters of Stamboul, it seemed as if mere
words could never express all I felt, and I
vainly struggled against my own incompetence
to render, in human language, the penetrating
charm surrounding me.

Here, on the contrary, words exact and
truthful in themselves seem always too thrilling,
too great for the subject; seem to embellish it
unduly. I feel as if I were acting for my own
benefit, some wretchedly trivial and third-rate
comedy; and whenever I try to consider my
home in a serious spirit, the scoffing figure of
M. Kangourou rises up before me, the matrimonial agent, to whom I am indebted for my
happiness.

IX.

YVES comes up to us whenever he is free, in the evening at five o'clock, after his work on board

He is our only European visitor, and with the exception of a few civilities and cups of tea, exchanged with our neighbours, we lead a very retired life. Only in the evenings, winding our way through the precipitous little streets and carrying our lanterns at the end of short sticks, we go down to Nagasaki in search of amusement at the theatres, at the "tea-houses," or in the bazaars.

Yves treats this wife of mine as if she were a plaything, and continually assures me that she is charming.

Myself, I find her as exasperating as the cicalas on my roof; and when I am alone at home, side by side with this little creature twanging the strings of her long-necked guitar, in front of this marvellous panorama of pagodas and mountains,—I am overcome by a sadness full of tears.

X.

LAST night, as we lay under the Japanese roof of Diou-djen-dji,—under the thin and ancient wooden roof scorched by a hundred years of sunshine, vibrating at the least sound, like the stretched-out parchment of a tamtam, —in the silence which prevails at two o'clock in the morning, we heard overhead a regular wild huntsman's chase passing at full galop :

" Nidzoumi ! " (" the mice ! "), said Chrysanthème.

Suddenly, the word brings back to my mind yet another, spoken in a very different language, in a country far away from here : " Setchan ! "

a word heard elsewhere, a word that has like-
wise been whispered in my ear by a woman's
voice, under similar circumstances, in a moment
of nocturnal terror—" Setchan ! " It was
during one of our first nights at Stamboul spent
under the mysterious roof of Eyoub, when
danger surrounded us on all sides ; a noise on
the steps of the black staircase had made us
tremble, and she also, my dear little Turkish
companion, had said to me in her beloved
language, " Setchan ! " (" the mice ! ").

At that fond recollection, a thrill of sweet
memories coursed through my veins ; it was as
though I had been startled out of a long ten
years' sleep ; I looked down upon the doll
beside me with a sort of hatred, wondering
why I was there, and I arose, with almost a
feeling of remorse, to escape from that blue
gauze net.

I stepped out upon the verandah, and there
I paused, gazing into the depths of the starlit
night. Beneath me Nagasaki lay asleep, wrapt
in a soft light slumber, hushed by the murmuring sound of a thousand insects in the moonlight, and fairylike with its roseate hues.
Then, turning my head, I saw behind me the
gilded idol with our lamps burning in front of
it ; the idol smiling its impassive Buddha

smile ; and its presence seemed to cast around it something, I know not what, strange and incomprehensible. Never until now had I slept under the eye of such a god.

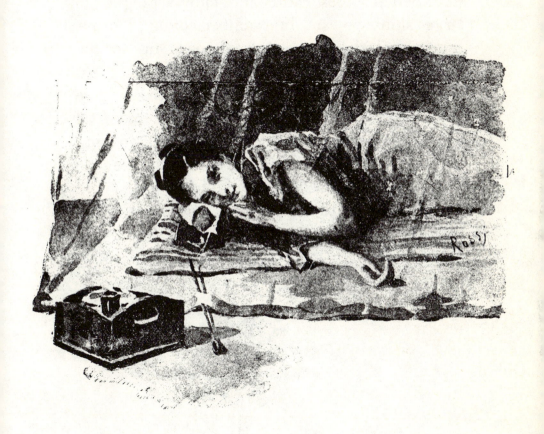

In the midst of the calm and silence of the night, I strove to recall my poignant impressions of Stamboul ; but alas, I strove in vain, they would not return to me in this strange, far-off

world. Through the transparent blue gauze
appeared my little Japanese, as she lay in her
sombre night-dress with all the fantastic grace
of her country, the nape of her neck resting on
its wooden block, and her hair arranged in
large shiny bows. Her amber-coloured arms,
pretty and delicate, emerged, bare up to the
shoulders, from her wide sleeves.

"What can those mice on the roof have
done to him?" thought Chrysanthème. Of
course she could not understand. In a coaxing
manner, like a playful kitten, she glanced at me
with her half-closed eyes, inquiring why I did
not come back to sleep,—and I returned to my
place by her side.

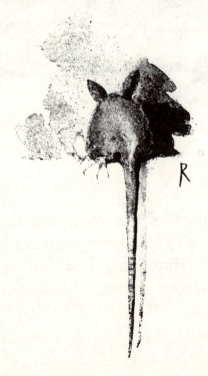

XI.

IT is the **National Fête day of France**. In Nagasaki roadstead, all the ships are dressed out with flags, and salutes are firing in our honour.

Alas! All day long, I cannot help thinking of that last fourteenth of July, spent in the deep calm and stillness of my old home, the door closed to all intruders, while the gay crowd roared outside; there I had remained till evening, seated on a bench, shaded by a trellis covered with honeysuckle, where in the byegone days of my childhood's summers, I used to settle myself with my copybooks and pretend to learn my lessons. Oh! those days when I was supposed to learn my lessons: how my thoughts used to rove,—what voyages, what distant lands, what tropical forests did I not behold in my dreams! At that time, near the garden bench, in some of the crevices in the stone wall, there dwelt many a big ugly black spider ever on the watch, peeping out of his nook ready to pounce upon any giddy fly or wandering centipede. One of my amusements consisted in tickling the spiders gently, very gently, with a blade of grass or a cherry stalk in their holes. Mystified, they would rush out, fancying they had to deal with some sort of prey, whilst I would rapidly draw back my hand in disgust. Well, last year, on that fourteenth of July, as I recalled my days of Latin themes and translations, now for ever flown, and this game of boyish days, I actually recognized the very same spiders (or at least their daughters), lying in wait in the very same holes. Gazing at them and at the tufts of grass and moss around me, a thousand memories of these summers of my early life welled up within me, memories which for years past had lain slumbering under this old wall, sheltered by the ivy boughs. While all that is ourselves perpetually changes and passes away, the constancy with which Nature repeats, always in the same manner, her most infinitesimal details, seems a wonderful mystery ; the same peculiar species of moss grow afresh for centuries on precisely the same spot, and the same little insects each summer do the same thing in the same place.

I must admit that this episode of my childhood and the spiders, have little to do with the story of Chrysanthème. But an incongruous interruption is quite in keeping with the taste of this country ; everywhere it is practised, in conversation, in music, even in painting ; a landscape painter, for instance, when he has finished a picture of mountains and crags, will not hesitate to draw in the very middle of the sky a circle, or a lozenge, or some kind of framework, within which he will represent anything incoherent and inappropriate : a bonze fanning himself, or a lady taking a cup of tea. Nothing is more thoroughly Japanese than such digressions made without the slightest àpropos.

Moreover, if I roused my past memories, it was the better to force myself to notice the difference between that 14th of July last year, so peacefully spent amidst surroundings familiar to me from my earliest infancy, and the present animated one, passed in the midst of such a novel world.

To-day, therefore, under the scorching midday sun, at two o'clock, three quick-footed djins dragged us at full speed,—Yves, Chrysanthème and myself,—in Indian file, each in a little jolting

cart, to the further end of Nagasaki, and there deposited us at the foot of some gigantic steps that run straight up into the mountain.

These are the granite steps leading to the great temple of Osueva; wide enough to give access to a whole regiment ; they are as grand and imposing as any work of Babylon or Nineveh, and in complete contrast with all the finical surroundings.

We climb up and up,—Chrysanthème listlessly, affecting fatigue, under her paper parasol painted with pink butterflies on a black ground. As we ascended, we passed under enormous monastic porticos, also in granite of rude and

primitive style.   In truth, these steps and these
temple porticos are the only imposing works
that this people has created, and they astonish,
for they scarcely seem Japanese.

We climb up still higher.   At this sultry hour
of the day, from top to bottom of the immense

grey steps, only we three are to be seen ; on all
that granite there are but the pink butterflies on
Chrysanthème's parasol, to throw a cheerful and
brilliant note.

We passed through the first temple yard, in
which are a couple of white china turrets, bronze

lanterns, and the statue of a large horse in jade. Then without pausing at the sanctuary, we turned to the left, and entered a shady garden, which formed a terrace halfway up the hill, and at the extremity of which was situated the *Donko-Tchaya*,—in English : the *tea-house of the Toads*.

It was here that Chrysanthème was taking us. We sat down at a table, under a black linen tent, decorated with large white letters (of funereal aspect), and two laughing *mousmés* hurried up to wait upon us.

The word *mousmé* means a young girl, or very young woman. It is one of the prettiest words in the Niponese language; it seems almost as if there were a little *moue* * in the very sound, and as if a pretty taking little pout such as they put on, and also a little pert physiognomy were described by it. I shall often make use of it, knowing none other in our own language that conveys the same meaning.

Some Japanese Watteau must have mapped out this *Donko-Tchaya*, for it has rather an affected air of rurality, though very pretty. Well shaded, under a thick vault of large trees densely foliaged, a miniature lake hard by, the

---

* *Moue* means "pout" in French.

chosen residence of a few toads, has given it its attractive denomination. Lucky toads, who crawl and croak on the finest of moss, in the midst of tiny artificial islets decked with gardenias in full bloom. From time to time, one of them informs us of his thoughts by a "Couac," uttered in a deep bass croak infinitely more hollow than that of our own toads.

Under the tent of this tea-house, we are as it were on a balcony jutting out from the mountain side, overhanging from on high the greyish town and its suburbs buried in greenery Around, above and beneath us cling and hang on every possible point, clumps of trees and fresh green woods, with the delicate and varying foliage of the temperate zone. Then we can see, at our feet, the deep roadstead, foreshortened and slanting, diminished in appearance till it looks like a terrible sombre tear in the mass of large green mountains; and further still, quite low down, on the waters which seem black and stagnant, are to be seen, very tiny and overwhelmed, the men-of-war, the steamboats and the junks, flags flying from every mast. On the dark green, which is the dominant shade around, stand out these thousand scraps of bunting, emblems of the different nationalities, all displayed, all flying in honour of far-distant France. The colours most prevailing in this motley assemblage are the white flag with a red ball, emblem of the *Empire of the Rising Sun,* where we now are.

With the exception of three or four mousmés at the further end who are practising with bows and arrows, we are to-day the only people in the garden, and the mountain round about is silent.

Having finished her cigarette and her cup of tea, Chrysanthème also wishes to exert her skill; for archery is still held in honour among the young women. The old man who keeps the range, picks out for her his best arrows tipped with white and red feathers,—and she takes aim with a serious air. The mark is a circle, traced in the middle of a picture on which is painted in flat grey tones, terrifying chimera flying through the clouds.

Chrysanthème is certainly an adroit marks-
woman, and we admire her as
much as she expected.

Then Yves, who is
usually clever at all
games of skill, wishes to
try his luck, and fails. It
is amusing to see her,
with her mincing ways
and smiles, arrange with
the tips of her little fingers, the sailor's broad
hands, placing them on
the bow and the string in
order to teach him the
proper manner. Never
have they seemed to get
on so well together, Yves
and my dolly, and I
might even feel anxious,
were I less sure of my
good brother, and if,
moreover, it were not a
matter of perfect indifference to me.

In the stillness of the garden, mid the balmy

peacefulness of these mountains, a loud noise suddenly startles us ; a unique, powerful, terrible sound, which is prolonged in infinite metallic vibrations. It begins again sounding more appalling : *Boum !* borne to us by the rising wind.

" *Nippon Kané !* " explains Chrysanthème, —and she again takes up her brightly-feathered arrows. " *Nippon Kané* (the Japanese brass); it is the Japanese brass that is sounding!" It is the monstrous gong of a monastery, situated in a suburb beneath us. Well, it is powerful indeed "the Japanese brass!" When the strokes are ended, when it is no longer heard, a vibration seems to linger among the suspended foliage, and an endless quiver runs through the air.

I am obliged to admit that Chrysanthème looks very charming shooting her arrows, her figure well bent back the better to bend her bow; her loose-hanging sleeves caught up to her shoulders, showing the graceful bare arms polished like amber and very much of the same colour. Each arrow whistles by with the rustle of a bird's wing,—then a short sharp little blow is heard, the target is hit, always.

At nightfall, when Chrysanthème has gone up to Diou-djen-dji, we cross, Yves and myself, the European concession, on our way to the ship, to take up our watch till the following day. The cosmopolitan quarter exhaling an odour of absinthe, is dressed up with flags, and squibs are being fired off in honour of France. Long lines of djins pass by, dragging as fast as their naked legs can carry them, the crew of the *Triomphante*, who are shouting and fanning themselves. The "Marseillaise" is heard everywhere; English sailors are singing it, gutturally with a dull and slow cadence like their own "God Save." In all the American bars, grinding organs are hammering it with many an odious variation and flourish. in order to attract our men.

Just one funny recollection comes back to me of that evening. On our return, we had by mistake got into a street inhabited by a multitude of ladies of doubtful reputation. I can still see that big fellow Yves, struggling with a whole band of tiny little mousmés of some twelve or fifteen years of age, who barely reached up to his waist, and were pulling him by the sleeves, anxious to lead him astray.

Astonished and indignant he repeated as he extricated himself from their clutches: "Oh, this is too much!" So shocked was he at seeing such mere babies, so young, so tiny, already so brazen and shameless.

XII.

THERE are now four of us, four officers of my ship, married like myself, and inhabiting the slopes of the same suburb. It is quite an ordinary occurrence, and is arranged without difficulties, mystery or danger, through the negotiations of the same M. Kangourou.

As a matter of course, we are on visiting terms with all these ladies.

First there is our very merry neighbour Madame Campanule, who is little Charles

N——'s wife; then Madame Jonquille, who is
even merrier than Campanule, like a young bird
and the daintiest fairy of the whole lot : she has
married X——, a fair northerner who adores
her; they are a loverlike and inseparable pair, the
only one that will probably weep when the hour
of parting comes. Then Sikou-San with Doctor
Y—— ; and lastly the midshipman Z—— with
the tiny Madame Touki-San, no taller than a
boot: thirteen years old at the outside and already
a regular woman, full of her own importance, a
petulant little gossip. In my childhood, I was
sometimes taken to the *Learned Animals*
Theatre, and I remember a certain Madame de
Pompadour, a principal rôle, filled by a gaily
dressed-up old monkey; Touki-San reminds
me of her.

In the evening, all these folk generally come
and fetch us for a long processional walk with
lighted lanterns. My wife, more serious, more
melancholy, perhaps even more refined, and
belonging, I fancy, to a higher class, tries when
these friends come to us to play the part of the
lady of the house. It is comical to see the entry
of these ill-matched couples, partners for a day,
the ladies with their disjointed bows falling on
all fours before Chrysanthème, the queen of
the establishment. When we are all assembled,

we start off, arm in arm, one behind the other,
and always carrying at the end of our short
sticks little white or red paper lanterns;—it
seems it is pretty.

We are obliged to scramble down the kind of
street, or rather goat's-path, which leads to the
Japanese Nagasaki,—with the prospect, alas! of
having to climb up again at night; clamber up
all the steps, all the slippery slopes, stumble over
all the stones, before we shall be able to get
home, go to bed, and sleep. We make our descent in the darkness, under the branches, under
the foliage, betwixt dark gardens and venerable
little houses that throw but a faint glimmer on
the road; and when the moon is absent or
clouded over, our lanterns are by no means un-
necessary.

When at last we reach the bottom, suddenly,
without transition, we find ourselves in the very
heart of Nagasaki and its busy throng in a long
illuminated street, where vociferating djins hurry
along and thousands of paper lanterns swing
and gleam in the wind. It is life and animation,
after the peace of our silent suburb.

Here, decorum requires we should separate
from our wives. All five take hold of each
others' hands, like a batch of little girls out

walking. We follow them with an air of indifference. Seen from behind, our dolls are really very dainty, with their back hair so tidily done

up, their tortoiseshell pins so coquettishly arranged. They shuffle along, their high wooden clogs making an ugly sound, striving to walk with their toes turned in, according to the height of fashion and elegance. At every minute they burst out laughing.

Yes, seen from behind, they are very pretty; they have, like all Japanese women, the most lovely turn of the head. Moreover, they are very funny, thus drawn up in line. In speaking of them, we say: " Our little dancing dogs," and in truth they are singularly like them.

'This great Nagasaki is the same from one end to another, with its numberless petroleum

lamps burning, its many - coloured lanterns flickering, and innumerable panting djins. Always the same narrow streets, lined on each side with the same low houses, built in paper and wood. Always the same shops, without glass windows, open to all the winds, equally rudimentary whatever may be sold or made in them; whether they display the finest gold lacquer ware, the most marvellous china jars, or old worn-out pots and pans, dried fish, and ragged frippery. All the salesmen are seated on the ground in the midst of their valuable or trumpery merchandise, their legs bared nearly to the waist. And all kinds of queer little trades are carried on under the public gaze, by strangely primitive means, by workmen of the most ingenuous type.

Oh! what wonderful goods are exposed for sale in those streets! what whimsical extravagances in those bazaars!

No horses, no carriages are ever seen in the town; nothing but people on foot, or the comical little carts dragged along by the run-

ners. Some few Europeans straggling hither
and thither, wanderers from the ships in harbour ; some Japanese (fortunately as yet but few

in number) dressed up in coats ; other natives
who content themselves with adding to their
national costume the pot hat, from which
their long sleek locks hang down ; and

all around, eager haggling, bargaining,—and laughter.

In the bazaars every evening our mousmés make endless purchases; like spoilt children they buy everything they fancy: toys, pins, ribbons, flowers. And then they prettily offer each other presents, with childish little smiles. For instance, Campanule buys for Chrysanthème an ingeniously contrived lantern on which, set in motion by some invisible machinery, Chinese shadows dance in a ring round the flame. In return, Chrysanthème gives Campanule a magic fan, with paintings that change at will from butterflies fluttering round cherry-blossoms, to outlandish monsters pursuing each other across black clouds. Touki offers Sikou a cardboard mask representing the bloated countenance of Daï-Cok, god of wealth; and Sikou replies by a long crystal trumpet, by means of which are produced the most extraordinary sounds, like a turkey gobbling. Everything is uncouth, fantastical to excess, grotesquely lugubrious; everywhere we are surprised by incomprehensible conceptions, which seem the work of distorted imaginations.

In the fashionable tea - houses where we finish up our evenings, the little servant-

girls now bow to us, on our arrival, with
an air of respectful recognition, as belonging
to the fast set of Nagasaki. There we carry
on desultory conversations, full of misunder-
standings and endless *quid pro quo's* of uncouth words,—in little gardens lighted up
with lanterns, near ponds full of gold fish,
with little bridges, little islets and little ruined
towers. They hand us tea and white and
pink-coloured sweetmeats flavoured with pepper
that taste strange and unfamiliar, and bever-
ages mixed with snow tasting of flowers or
perfumes.

To give a faithful account of those evenings,
would require a more affected style than our
own ; and some kind of graphic sign would
have also to be expressly invented and scattered
at haphazard amongst the words, indicating the
moment at which the reader should laugh,—
rather a forced laugh, perhaps, but amiable and
gracious. The evening at an end ; it is time
to return up there.

Oh ! that street, that road, that we must
clamber up every evening, under the starlit sky,
or the heavy thunder-clouds, dragging by the

hand our drowsy mousmé in order to regain
our home perched on high half-way up the hill,
where our bed of matting awaits us.

XIII.

THE cleverest amongst us has been Louis de
S——. Having formerly inhabited Japan, and
made a marriage Japan fashion there, he is now
satisfied to remain the friend of our wives, of
whom he has become the *Komodachi taksan
takaï, the very tall friend* (as they say on
account of his excessive height and slender-
ness). Talking Japanese more freely than we
can, he is their confidential adviser, disturbs

or reconciles at will our households, and has infinite amusement at our expense.

This *very tall friend* of our wives enjoys all the fun that these little creatures can give him, without any of the worries of domestic life. With brother Yves, and little Oyouki (the daughter of Madame Prune, my landlady,) he makes up our incongruous party.

XIV.

M. Sucre and Madame Prune,* my landlord and wife, two perfectly unique personages but recently escaped from the panel of some screen, live below us on the ground floor; and very old they seem to have this daughter of fifteen, Oyouki, who is Chrysanthème's inseparable friend.

Both of them are entirely absorbed in the practices of Shintoist devotion: perpetually on their knees before their family altar, perpetually occupied in murmuring their lengthy orisons to the Spirits, and clapping their hands from time to time to recall around them the inattentive essences floating in the atmosphere;—in their spare moments they cultivate in little pots of

* In Japanese: *Sato-san* and *Oumé- an*.

gaily-painted earthenware, dwarf shrubs and unheard-of flowers which smell deliciously in the evening.

M. Sucre is taciturn, dislikes society, looks like a mummy in his blue cotton dress. He writes a great deal, (his memoirs, I fancy) with a paint-brush held in his finger-tips, on long strips of rice-paper of a faint grey tint.

Madame Prune is eagerly attentive, obsequious and rapacious ; her eye-brows are closely shaven, her teeth carefully lacquered with black as befits a lady of gentility, and at all and no matter what hours, she appears on all fours at the entrance of our apartment, to offer us her services.

As to Oyouki, she rushes upon us ten times a day,—whether we are sleeping, or dressing,— like a whirlwind on a visit, flashing upon us, a very gust of dainty youthfulness and droll gaiety, —a living peal of laughter. She is round of figure, round of face ; half baby, half girl ; and so affectionate that she bestows kisses on the slightest occasion with her great puffy lips, — a little moist, it is true, like a child's, but nevertheless very fresh and very red.

XV.

In our dwelling, open as it is all the night through, the lamps burning before the gilded Buddha procure us the company of the insect inhabitants of every garden in the neighbourhood. Moths, mosquitoes, cicalas, and other extraordinary insects of which I don't even know the names,—all this company assembles around us.

It is extremely funny, when some unexpected grasshopper, some free-and-easy beetle presents

itself without invitation or excuse, scampering
over our white mats, to see the manner in which
Chrysanthème indicates it to my righteous
vengeance,—merely pointing her finger at it,
without another word than " Hou ! " said with
bent head, a particular pout, and a scandalized
air.

There is a fan kept expressly for the purpose
of blowing them out of doors again.

XVI.

HERE, I must own, that to the reader of my story it must appear to drag a little.

In default of exciting intrigues and tragic adventures, I would fain have known how to infuse into it a little of the sweet perfumes of the gardens which surround me, something of the gentle warmth of the sunshine, of the shade of these graceful trees. Love being wanting, I should like it to breathe of the restful tranquillity of this far-away suburb. Then, too, I should like it to re-echo the sound of Chrysanthème's guitar, in which I begin to find a certain charm, for want of something better, in the silence of the lovely summer evenings.

All through these moonlit nights of July, the weather has been calm, luminous and magnificent. Ah! what glorious clear nights, what exquisite roseate tints beneath that wonderful moon, what mystery of blue shadows in the thick tangle of trees. And, from the heights where stood our verandah, how prettily the town lay sleeping at our feet!

After all, I do not positively detest this little Chrysanthème, and when there is no repugnance on either side, habit turns into a makeshift of attachment.

XVII.

ALWAYS, over, in, and through everything, rises day and night from this Japanese landscape the song of the cicalas, ceaseless, strident, and prodigious. It is everywhere, and neverending, at no matter what hour of the burning day, what hour of the cool and refreshing night. In the midst of the roads, as we approached our anchorage, we had heard it at the same time from the two shores, from both walls of green mountains. It is wearisome and haunting; it seems to be the manifestation, the noise expressive of the special kind of life peculiar to this region of the world. It is the voice of summer in these islands; it is the song of unconscious rejoicing, always content with itself and always appearing to inflate, to rise upwards, in a greater and greater exultation at the sheer happiness of living.

It is to me the noise characteristic of this country,—this, and the cry of the falcon, which had in like manner greeted our entry into Japan. Over the valleys and the deep bay sail these birds, uttering from time to time their three cries, "Han! han! han!" in a key of sadness, which seems the extreme of painful astonishment. And the mountains around re-echo their cry.

XVIII.

Yves, Chrysanthème, and little Oyouki have
struck up a friendship so great that it amuses
me : I even think, that in my home life, this
intimacy is what affords me the greatest enter-
tainment.   They form a contrast which gives
rise to the most absurd jokes, and most unfore-
seen situations.   He brings into this fragile
little paper house, his sailor's freedom and ease
of manner, and his Breton accent ; side by side
with these tiny mousmés of affected manners

and bird-like voices, who, small as they are, rule the big fellow as they please; make him eat with chopsticks; teach him Japanese "*pigeon-vole*,"—and cheat him, and quarrel, and almost die of laughter over it all.

Certainly he and Chrysanthème take a pleasure in each other's company. But I remain serenely undisturbed, and cannot imagine that this little chance doll with whom I play at married life, could possibly bring a serious trouble between this " brother " and myself.

XIX.

My family of Japanese relations, very numerous and very conspicuous, is a great source of diversion to those of my brother officers who visit me in my villa on the hill,—most especially to *komodachi taksan takaï (the immensely tall friend)*.

I have a charming mother-in-law—quite a woman of the world,—little sisters-in-law, little cousins, and aunts who are still quite young.

I have even a poor cousin, twice removed, who is a djin. There was some hesitation in owning this latter to me ; but, behold ! during the ceremony of introduction, we exchanged a smile of recognition, it was number 415.

Over this poor 415, my friends on board crack no end of jokes,—one in particular, who, less than any one has the right to make them, little Charles N——, for his mother-in-law was once a porter, or something of the kind, at the gateway of a pagoda.

I, however, who have a great respect for strength and agility, much appreciate this new relative of mine. His legs are undoubtedly the best in all Nagasaki, and whenever I am in a hurry, I always beg Madame Prune to send down to the djin stand, and engage my cousin.

XX.

I ARRIVED unexpectedly to-day at Diou-djen-dji, in the midst of a burning noonday heat. At the foot of the stairs lay Chrysanthème's wooden clogs and her sandals of varnished leather.

In our rooms, up above, all was open to the air; bamboo blinds lowered on the sunny side, and through their transparency came warm air and golden threads of light. To-day, the flowers Chrysanthème had placed in our bronze vases were lotus, and my eyes fell, as I entered, upon their great rosy cups.

According to her usual custom, she was lying flat on the floor enjoying her daily siesta.

What a singular originality these bouquets of Chrysanthème always have: a something difficult to define, a Japanese slimness, a mannered grace which we should never succeed in imparting to them.

She was sleeping flat on her face upon the mats, her high headdress and tortoiseshell pins standing out boldly from the rest of the horizontal figure. The train of her tunic prolonged her delicate little body, like the tail of a bird; her arms were stretched crosswise, the sleeves spread out like wings,—and her long guitar lay beside her.

She looked like a dead fairy; or still more did she resemble some great blue dragon-fly, which, having alighted on that spot, some unkind hand had pinned to the floor.

Madame Prune, who had come upstairs after me, always officious and eager, manifested by her gestures her sentiments of indignation on beholding the careless reception accorded by

Chrysanthème to her lord and master, and advanced to wake her.

"Pray do nothing of the kind, my good Madame Prune, you don't know how much I prefer her like that!" I had left my shoes

below, according to custom, by the side of the little clogs and sandals; and I entered on the tips of my toes, very, very softly, to go and sit awhile under the verandah.

What a pity this little Chrysanthème cannot always be asleep; she is really extremely decorative seen in this manner,—and like this, at least, she does not bore me. Who knows what may perchance be going on in that little head and heart! If I only had the means of finding out! But strange to say, since we have kept house together, instead of pushing my studies in the Japanese language further, I have neglected them, so much have I felt the utter impossibility of ever interesting myself in the subject.

Seated under my verandah, my eyes wandered over the temples and cemeteries spread at my feet, over the woods and green mountains, over Nagasaki lying bathed in the sunlight. The cicalas were chirping their loudest, the strident noise trembling feverishly in the hot air. All was calm, full of light and full of heat.

Nevertheless, to my taste, it is not yet enough so! What then can have changed upon the earth? The burning noon-days of summer, such as I can recall in days gone by, were more brilliant, more full of sunshine; Nature seemed to me in those days more powerful, more terrible. One would say this was only a pale copy of all that I knew in early years,—a copy in which something is wanting. Sadly do I ask myself,—Is the splendour of the summer only this? *was it* only this? or is it the fault of my eyes, and as time goes on shall I behold everything around me paling still more?

Behind me a faint and melancholy strain of music,—melancholy enough to make one shiver,—and shrill, shrill as the song of the grasshoppers, began to make itself heard, very softly at first, then growing louder and rising in the silence of the noonday like the diminutive wail of some poor Japanese soul in pain and anguish; it was Chrysanthème and her guitar awaking together.

It pleased me that the idea should have occurred to her to greet me with music, instead of eagerly hastening to wish me "Good morning." (At no time have I ever given myself the trouble to pretend the slightest affection for her, and a certain coldness even has grown up between us, especially when we are alone.) But to-day I turn to her with a smile, and wave my hand for her to continue. "Go on, it amuses me to listen to your quaint little impromptu." It is singular that the music of this essentially merry people should be so plaintive. But undoubtedly that which Chrysanthème is playing at this moment is worth listening to. Whence can it have come to her? What unutterable dreams, for ever hidden from me, fly through her yellow head, when she plays or sings in this manner?

Suddenly: Pan, pan, pan! Someone

knocks three times, with a harsh and bony
finger against one of the steps of our stairs,
and in the aperture of our doorway appears an
idiot, clad in a suit of grey tweed, who bows
low. "Come in, come in, M. Kangourou.
How well you come, just in the nick of time!
I was actually becoming enthusiastic over your
country!"

It was a little washing bill, which M.
Kangourou respectfully wished to hand to me,
with a profound bend of the whole body, the
correct pose of the hands on the knees, and a
long snake-like hiss.

XXI.

FOLLOWING the road which climbs past the front of our dwelling, one passes a dozen or more old villas, a few garden walls, and then there is nothing but the lonely mountain side, with little paths winding upwards towards the summit through plantations of tea, bushes of camellias, underwood and rocks. The mountains round Nagasaki are covered with cemeteries ; for centuries and centuries past it is up here they have brought their dead.

But there is neither sadness nor horror in these Japanese sepulchres ; it would seem as if among this frivolous and childish people, death itself could not be taken seriously. The monuments are either Buddhas, in granite, seated on lotus, or upright funereal stones with an inscription in gold; they are grouped together in little enclosures in the midst of the woods, or on natural terraces delightfully situated, and are generally reached by long stairways of stone carpeted with moss; from time to time, these pass under one of the sacred gateways, of which the shape, always the same, rude and simple, is a smaller reproduction of those in the temples.

Up above us, the tombs of our mountain are of so hoary an antiquity that they no longer alarm any one, even by night. It is a region of forsaken cemeteries. The dead hidden away there have long since become one with the earth around them; and these thousands of little grey stones, these multitudes of ancient little Buddhas, eaten away by lichens, seem to be now no more than a proof of a series of existences, long anterior to our own, and lost for ever and altogether in the mysterious depths of ages.

XXII.

CHRYSANTHÈME'S meals are something in-describable.

She begins in the morning, when she wakes, by two little green wild plums pickled in vinegar and rolled in powdered sugar. A cup of tea completes this almost traditional breakfast of Japan, the very same Madame Prune is eating down-stairs, the same served up to travellers in the inns.

During the course of the day the feeding is continued by two little dinners of the drollest composition. They are brought up on a tray of red lacquer, in microscopic cups with covers, from Madame Prune's apartment, where they are cooked: a hashed sparrow, a stuffed prawn, sea-weed with a sauce, a salt sweetmeat, a sugared chili. Chrysanthème tastes a little of all, with

dainty pecks and the aid of her little chopsticks, raising the tips of her fingers with affected grace. At every dish she makes a face, leaves three parts of it, and dries her finger-tips after it in apparent disgust.

These menus vary according to the inspiration which may have seized Madame Prune. But one thing never varies, either in our household or in any other, neither in the north nor in the south of the Empire, and that is the dessert and the manner of eating it : after all these little dishes, which are a mere make-believe, is brought in a wooden bowl, bound with copper,—an enormous bowl, fit for Gargantua, and filled to the very brim with rice, plainly cooked in water. Chrysanthème fills another large bowl from it (sometimes twice, sometimes three times), darkens its snowy whiteness with a black sauce flavoured with fish which is contained in a delicately shaped blue cruet, mixes it all together, carries the bowl to her lips, and crams down all the rice, shovelling it with her two chopsticks into her very throat. Next the little cups and covers are picked up, as well as the tiniest crumb that may have fallen upon the white mats, the irreproachable purity of which nothing is allowed to tarnish. And so ends the dinner.

XXIII.

Down below in the town, a street singer had established herself in a little thoroughfare; people had collected around her to listen to her singing, and we three—that is, Yves, Chrysanthème and I—who chanced to be passing, stopped like others.

Quite young, rather fat, fairly pretty, she strummed her guitar and sang, rolling her eyes fiercely, like a virtuoso executing feats of difficulty. She lowered her head, stuck her chin

into her neck, in order to draw deeper notes
from the furthermost recesses of her body ; and
succeeded in bringing forth a great hoarse voice,
—a voice that might have belonged to an aged
frog, a ventriloquist's voice, coming from whence
it would be impossible to say (this is the best
stage manner, the final word of art, for the in-
terpretation of tragic pieces).

Yves cast an indignant glance upon her :

" Good gracious," said he, " it's the voice
of a—" (words failed him, in his astonishment)
" it's the voice of a—a monster ! "

And he looked at me, almost frightened by
this little being, and anxious to know what I
thought of it.

My poor Yves was out of temper on this
occasion, because I had induced him to come
out in a straw hat with a turned-up brim, which
did not please him.

" It suits you remarkably well, Yves, I
assure you."

" Oh, indeed ! You say so, you. For my
part, I think it looks like a magpie's nest ! "

As a fortunate diversion from the singer and
the hat, here comes a cortège, advancing
towards us from the end of the street, something

remarkably like a funeral. Bonzes march in front dressed in robes of black gauze, having much the appearance of Catholic priests; the principal personage of the procession, the corpse, comes last, laid in a sort of little closed palanquin which is daintily pretty. This is followed by a band of mousmés, hiding their laughing faces beneath a kind of veil, and carrying in vases of the sacred shape the artificial lotus with silver petals indispensable at a funeral; then come fine ladies, on foot, smirking and stifling a wish to laugh, beneath parasols on which are painted in the gayest colours, butterflies and storks.

Now they are quite close to us, we must stand back to give them room. Chrysanthème all at once assumes a suitable air of gravity, and Yves bares his head, taking off the magpie's nest.

Yes, it is true, it is death that is passing by!

I had almost lost sight of the fact, so little does this recall it.

The procession will climb high up, far away above Nagasaki, into the heart of the green mountain all peopled with tombs. There the poor fellow will be laid at rest, with his palanquin above him, and his vases and his flowers of silvered paper. Well, at least the poor defunct will lie in a charming spot commanding a lovely view.

They will now return half laughing, half snivelling, and to-morrow no one will think of it again.

XXIV.

THE *Triomphante*, which has been lying in the roadsteads almost at the foot of the hill on which stands my house, enters the dock to-day to undergo repairs rendered necessary by the long blockade of Formosa.

I am now a long way from my home, and obliged to cross by boat the whole breadth of the bay when I wish to see Chrysanthème; for the dock is situated on the shore opposite to Diou-djen-dji. It is sunk in a little valley, narrow and deep, midst all kinds of foliage,—

bamboos, camellias, trees of all sorts; our masts and spars, seen from the deck, look as if they were tangled among the branches.

The situation of the vessel—no longer afloat —gives the crew a greater facility for clandestine escapes from the ship at no matter what hour of the night, and our sailors have made friends with all the girls of the villages perched on the mountains above us.

These quarters and his excessive liberty, give me some uneasiness about my poor Yves; for this country of frivolous pleasure has a little turned his head. Moreover, I am more and more convinced that he is in love with Chrysanthème.

It is really a pity that the sentiment has not occurred to me instead, since it is I who have gone the length of marrying her.

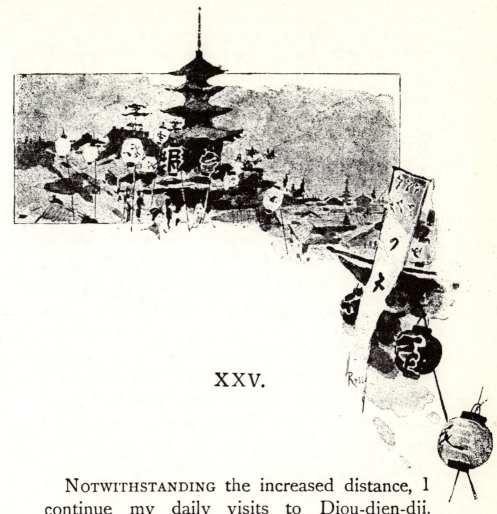

XXV.

Notwithstanding the increased distance, I continue my daily visits to Diou-djen-dji. When night has fallen, and the four couples who compose our society have joined us, as well as Yves and the *amazingly tall friend*,—we descend again into the town, stumbling by lantern light down the steep stairways and slopes of the old suburb.

This nocturnal stroll is always the same, and accompanied always by the same amuse-

ments : we pause before the same queer
stalls, we drink the same sugared drinks served
to us in the same little gardens. But our
troop is often more numerous : to begin with,
we chaperon Oyouki who is confided to our care
by her parents ; then we have two cousins of
my wife's—pretty little creatures ; and lastly
friends—guests of sometimes only ten or twelve
years old, little girls of the neighbourhood to
whom our mousmés wish to show some politeness.

Oh ! what a singular company of tiny beings
forms our suite and follows us into the tea-
gardens in the evenings ! The most absurd
faces, with sprigs of flowers stuck in the oddest
fashion in their comical and childish heads !
One might suppose it was a whole school of
mousmés out for an evening's frolic under our
care.

Yves returns with us, when time comes
to remount our hill,—Chrysanthème heaves
great sighs like a tired child, and stops on
every step, leaning on our arms.

When we have reached our destination he
says goodnight, just touches Chrysanthème's
hand, and descending once more, by the slope
which leads to the quays and the shipping, he

crosses the roadstead in a sampan, to get on board the *Triomphante.*

Meantime, we, with the aid of a sort of secret key, open the door of our garden, where Madame Prune's pots of flowers, ranged in the darkness, send forth delicious odours in the night air. We cross the garden by moonlight or starlight, and mount to our own rooms.

If it is very late,—a frequent occurrence,— we find all our wooden panels drawn and tightly shut by the careful M. Sucre (as a precaution against thieves), and our apartment is as close and as private as if it were a real European one.

In this house, when every chink is thus closed, a strange odour mingles with the musk and the lotus,—an odour essential to Japan, to the yellow race, belonging to the soil or emanating from the venerable woodwork ; almost an odour of wild beast. The mosquito curtain of dark blue gauze ready hung for the night, falls from the ceiling with the air of a mysterious velum. The gilded Buddha smiles eternally at the night-lamps burning before him ; some great moth, a constant frequenter of the house, which during the day sleeps clinging to our ceiling, flutters at this hour under the very nose of the god, turning and flitting round the thin quivering flames. And, motionless on the wall, its feelers spread out starwise, sleeps some great garden spider, which one must not kill because it is night. "Hou!" says Chrysanthème indignantly, pointing it out to me with levelled finger. "Quick! where is the fan kept for the purpose, wherewith to hunt it out of doors?"

Around us reigns a silence which is almost painful after all the joyous noises of the town, and all the laughter, now hushed, of our band of mousmés,—a silence of the country, of some sleeping village.

XXVI.

THE noise of the innumerable wooden panels
which at the fall of night are pulled and shut in
every Japanese house, is one of the peculiarities
of the country which will remain longest im-
printed on my memory.   From our neighbours'
houses, floating to us over the green gardens,
these noises reach us one after the other, in series,
more or less deadened, more or less distant.

Just below us, those of Madame Prune move
very badly, creak and make a hideous noise in
their worn-out grooves.

Ours are somewhat noisy too, for the old
house is full of echoes, and there are at least
twenty to run over long slides in order to close
in completely the kind of open hall in which
we live. Generally, it is Chrysanthème who
undertakes this piece of household work, and a
great deal of trouble it gives her, for she often
pinches her fingers in the singular awkwardness
of her too tiny hands, which have never been
accustomed to do any work.

Then comes her toilette for the night. With
a certain grace she lets fall the day-dress, and
slips on a more simple one of blue cotton, which
has the same pagoda sleeves, the same shape
all but the train, and which she fastens round
her waist by a sash of muslin of the same
colour.

The high head-dress remains untouched, it is
needless to say ; all but the pins which are taken
out and laid beside her in a lacquer box.

Then there is the little silver pipe that must
absolutely be smoked before going to sleep ;
this is one of the customs which most provokes
me, but has to be borne.

Chrysanthème, like a gipsy, squats before
a particular square box, made of red wood,
which contains a little tobacco jar, a little porcelain stove full of hot embers, and finally a little

bamboo pot serving at the same time as ash-
tray and spittoon.   (Madame P.une's smoking-
box downstairs, and every smoking-box in
Japan, both of men and women, is exactly the
same, and contains precisely the same objects,
arranged in precisely the same manner; and
wherever it may be, whether in the house of
the rich or the poor, it always lies about somewhere on the floor.)

The word " pipe " is at once too trivial and
too big to be applied to this delicate silver tube,
which is perfectly straight and at the end of
which, in a microscopic receptacle, is placed one
pinch of golden tobacco, chopped finer than
silken thread.

Two puffs, or at most three; it lasts scarcely
a few seconds, and the pipe is finished.   Then
pan, pan, pan, pan, the little tube is struck
smartly against the edge of the smoking-box to
knock out the ashes, which never will fall;
and this tapping, heard everywhere, in every
house, at every hour of the day or night, quick
and droll as the scratching of a monkey, is in
Japan one of the noises most characteristic of
human life.

" Anata nomimasé ! " (" You must smoke
too !") says Chrysanthème.

Having again filled the vexatious little pipe,

she puts the silver tube to my lips with a bow. Courtesy forbids my refusal ; but I find it detestably bitter.

Now, before laying myself down under the blue mosquito-net, I open two of the panels in the room, one on the side of the silent and  deserted footpath, the other one on the garden side, overlooking the terraces, so that the night air may breathe upon us, even at the risk of bringing us the company of some belated cockchafer, or more giddy moth.

Our wooden house, with its thin old walls, vibrates at night like a great dry fiddle ; the slightest noises grow great in it, become disfigured and positively disquieting.

Beneath the verandah are hung two little Æolian harps, which at the least ruffle of the breeze running through their blades of grass, emit a gentle tinkling sound, like the harmonious murmur of a brook ; outside, to the very furthest limits of the distance, the cicalas continue their great and everlasting concert ; over our heads, on the black roof, is heard passing like a witch's sabbath, the raging battle to the death of cats, rats and owls.

Presently, when in the early dawn, a fresher

breeze, mounting upwards from the sea and the deep harbour, reaches us, Chrysanthème will slyly get up and shut the panels I have opened.

Before that, however, she will have risen at least three times to smoke : having yawned like a cat, stretched herself, twisted in every direction her little amber arms, and her graceful little hands, she sits up resolutely, with all the waking groans and half words of a child, pretty and fascinating enough; then she emerges from the gauze tent, fills her little pipe, and breathes a few puffs of the bitter and unpleasant mixture.

Then comes *pan, pan, pan, pan*, against the box to shake out the ashes. In the resounding sonority of the night it makes quite a terrible noise, which wakes Madame Prune. This is fatal. Madame Prune is at once seized also with a longing to smoke which may not be denied; then, to the noise from above, comes an answering *pan, pan, pan, pan*, from below, exactly like it, exasperating and inevitable as an echo.

XXVII.

MORE cheerful are the noises of the morning : the cocks crowing, the wooden panels all round the neighbourhood sliding back upon their rollers; or the strange cry of some little fruit-hawker, patrolling our lofty suburb in the early dawn. And the grasshoppers absolutely seem to chirp more loudly, to celebrate the return of the sunlight.

Above all, rises to our ears from below the sound of Madame Prune's long prayers, ascend-

ing through the floor, monotonous as the song
of a somnambulist, regular and soothing as the
plash of a fountain. It lasts three-quarters of
an hour at least ; it drones along, a rapid flow
of words in a high nasal key ; from time to
time, when the inattentive Spirits are not
listening, it is accompanied by a clapping of dry
palms, or by harsh sounds from a kind of
wooden clapper made of two discs of mandragora
root ; it is an uninterrupted stream of prayer ; its
flow never ceases, and the quavering continues
without stopping, like the bleating of an old
nanny-goat in delirium.

"*After having washed the hands and feet,*" say
the sacred books, "*the great God Ama-Térace-
Omi-Kami, who is the royal power of Japan,
must be invoked; the manes of all the defunct
Emperors descended from him must also be invoked; next, the manes of all his personal
ancestors, to the furthest generation; the Spirits
of the Air and Sea; the Spirits of all secret and
impure places; the Spirits of the tombs of the
district whence you spring, etc., etc.*"

" I worship and implore you," sings Madame
Prune, "Oh Ama - Térace - Omi - Kami, royal
power. Cease not to protect your faithful
people, who are ready to sacrifice themselves
for their country. Grant that I may become as

holy as yourself, and drive from my mind all dark thoughts. I am a coward and a sinner : purge me from my cowardice and sinfulness, even as the north wind drives the dust into the sea. Wash me clean from all my iniquities, as one washes away uncleanness in the river of Kamo. Make me the richest woman in the world. I believe in your glory, which shall be spread over the whole earth, and illuminate it for ever for my happiness. Grant me the continued good health of my family, and above all, my own, who, oh Ama-Térace-Omi-Kami, do worship and adore you, and only you, etc., etc."

Here follow all the Emperors, all the Spirits, and the interminable list of the ancestors.

In her trembling old woman's falsetto, Madame Prune sings out all this, without omitting anything, at a pace which almost takes away her breath.

And very strange it is to hear : at length it seems hardly a human voice ; it sounds like a series of magic formulas, unwinding themselves from an inexhaustible roller, and escaping to take flight through the air. By its very weirdness, and by the persistency of its incantation, it ends by producing in my scarcely awakened brain, an almost religious impression.

Every day I wake to the sound of this

Shintoist litany chanted beneath me, vibrating through the exquisite clearness of the summer mornings,—while our night-lamps burn low before the smiling Buddha, while the eternal sun, scarcely risen, already sends through the cracks of our wooden panels its bright rays, which dart like golden arrows through our darkened dwelling and our blue gauze tent.

This is the moment at which I must rise, descend hurriedly to the sea by grassy footpaths all wet with dew, and so regain my ship.

Alas! in the days gone by, it was the cry of the muezzin which used to awaken me in the dark winter mornings, in far-away night-shrouded Stamboul.   *   *   *   *

XXVIII.

CHRYSANTHÈME has brought but few things with her, knowing that our married life would be of short duration.

She has placed her dresses and her fine sashes in little closed recesses, hidden in one of the walls of our apartment (the north wall, the only one of the four which will not take to pieces). The doors of these niches are white paper panels; the standing shelves and inside partitions, consisting of light woodwork, are put together in too finical a manner, too ingenious a way, giving rise to suspicions of secret drawers and conjuring tricks. We only put there things without any value, having a vague feeling that the cupboards themselves might spirit them away.

The box in which Chrysanthème stores away her gewgaws and letters, is one of the things that amuses me the most ; it is of English origin, in tin, and bears on its cover the coloured representation of some manufactory in the neighbourhood of London. Of course, it is as an exotic work of art, as a precious knick-knack, that Chrysanthème prefers it to any of her other boxes in lacquer or inlaid work. It contains all that a mousmé requires for her correspondence : Indian ink, a paintbrush, very thin grey tinted paper, cut up in long narrow strips, and funnily shaped envelopes, into which these strips are slipped (after having been folded up in some thirty folds) ; the envelopes being ornamented with pictures of landscapes, fishes, crabs, or birds.

On some old letters addressed to her, I can make out the two characters that represent her name : "Kikou-San" (Chrysanthème, Madame). And when I question her, she replies in Japanese, with an air of importance :

"My dear creature, they are letters from my female friends."

Oh! those friends of Chrysanthème, what funny little faces they have! That same box contains their portraits, their photographs stuck

on visiting cards, which are printed on the back with the name of Uyeno, the fashionable photographer in Nagasaki,—little creatures fit only to figure daintily on painted fans, and who have striven to assume a dignified attitude when once their necks have been placed in the headrest, and they have been told : " Now don't move."

It would really amuse me to read her friends' letters,—and above all my mousmé's answers.

XXIX.

THIS evening it rained heavily, and the night was thick and black. At about ten o'clock, on our return from one of the fashionable tea-houses we constantly frequent, we arrived,—Yves, Chrysanthème and myself,—at the certain familiar angle of the principal street, the certain turn where we must take leave of the lights and noises of the town, to clamber up the black steps and steep lanes which lead to our home at Diou-djen-dji.

There, before beginning our ascension, we must first buy lanterns from an old tradeswoman called Madame Très-Propre,* whose faithful customers we are. It is amazing what a quantity of these paper lanterns we consume. They are invariably decorated in the same way, with

painted night-moths or bats; fastened to the ceiling at the further end cf the shop, they hang in enormous clusters, and the old woman, seeing us arrive, gets upon a table to take them down. Grey or red are our usual choice; Madame Très - Propre knows our preferences and leaves the green or blue lanterns aside. But it is always hard work to unhook one, on account of the little short sticks by which they are held, and the strings by which they are tied getting entangled together. In an exaggerated pantomime, Madame Très-Propre expresses her despair at wasting so much of our valuable time : oh! if it only depended on her personal efforts! but ah, for the natural perversity of inanimate

* In Japanese : *O Séi-San*

things which have no consideration for human
dignity. With monkeyish antics, she even deems
it her duty to threaten the lanterns and shake

her fist at these inextricably tangled strings
which have the presumption to delay us.

It is all very well, but we know this

manœuvre by heart ; and if the old lady loses patience, so do we. Chrysanthème, who is half asleep, is seized with a fit of kitten-like yawning which she does not even trouble to hide behind her hand, and which appears to be endless. She pulls a very long face, at the thought of the steep hill we must struggle up to-night through the pelting rain.

I have the same feeling, and am thoroughly annoyed.

To what purpose, good heavens, do I clamber up every evening to that suburb, when it offers me no attraction whatever ?

The rain increases, what are we to do ? Outside, djins pass rapidly by, calling out : " Take care!" splashing the foot-passengers and casting through the shower, streams of light from their many-coloured lanterns. Mousmés and elderly ladies pass by, tucked up, muddy, laughing nevertheless, under their paper umbrellas, exchanging greetings, clacking their wooden pattens on the stone pavement ; the whole street is filled with the noise of the pattering feet and pattering rain.

As good luck will have it, at the same moment passes 415, our poor relative, who, seeing our distress, stops and promises to help us out of our difficulty ; as soon as he has de-

posited on the quay an Englishman he is conveying, he will come to our aid and bring all
that is necessary to relieve us from our lament-
able situation.

At last our lantern is unhooked, lighted, and
paid for. There is another shop opposite, where
we stop every evening; it is Madame L'Heure's,*
the woman who sells waffles ; we always buy a
provision from her, to refresh us on the way.
A very lively young woman is this pastry-cook,
and most anxious to make herself agreeable :
she looks quite like a screen picture, behind her
piled-up cakes, ornamented with little posies
We will take shelter under her roof while we
wait ; and, to avoid the drops that fall heavily
from the water-spouts, wedge ourselves tightly
against her display of white and pink sweetmeats, so artistically spread out on fresh and
delicate branches of cypress.

Poor 415, what a providence he is to us !
Already he re-appears, most excellent cousin,
ever smiling, ever running, while the water
streams down his handsome bare legs ; he brings
us two umbrellas, borrowed from a China
merchant, who is also a distant relative of ours.
Like me, Yves has till now never consented to

* In Japanese : *Tôki-San.*

use such a thing, but he now accepts one because
it is droll : in paper, of course, with innumerable
folds waxed and gummed, and the inevitable
flight of storks forming a wreath all round.

Chrysanthème, yawning more and more in
her kitten-like fashion, becomes coaxing in order
to be helped along, and tries to take my arm :

" I beg you, mousmé, this evening to take
the arm of Yves-San ; I am sure that will suit
us all three."

And there they go, she, tiny figure, hanging
on to the big fellow, and so they climb up. I
lead the way, carrying the lantern that lights
our steps, and whose flame I protect as well as
I can under my fantastic umbrella. On each
side of the road is heard the roaring torrent of
stormy waters rolling down from the mountain
side. To-night the way seems long, difficult
and slippery ; a succession of interminable
flights of steps, gardens and houses piled up one
above another ; waste lands, and trees which in
the darkness shake their dripping foliage on
our heads.

One would say that Nagasaki is ascending at
the same time as ourselves ; but yonder, and
very far away, in a kind of vapoury mist which
seems luminous on the blackness of the sky ;
and from the town there rises a confused

murmur of voices and rumbling of gongs and laughter.

The summer rain has not yet refreshed the atmosphere. On account of the stormy heat, the little suburban houses have been left open like sheds, and we can see all that is going on. Lamps ever lighted burn before the altars dedicated to Buddha and to the souls of the ancestors; but all good Niponese have already lain down to rest. Under the traditional tents of bluish-green gauze, we can see them, stretched out in rows by whole families; they are either sleeping, or hunting the mosquitoes, or fanning themselves. Niponese men and women, Niponese babies too, lying side by side with their parents; each one, young or old, in his little dark-blue cotton night-dress, and with his little wooden block to rest the nape of his neck.

A few houses are open, where amusements are still going on; here and there, from the sombre gardens, the sound of a guitar reaches our ears, some dance giving in its weird rhythm a strange impression of sadness.

Here is the well, surrounded by bamboos, where we are wont to make a nocturnal halt for Chrysanthème to take breath. Yves begs me to throw forward the red gleam of my lantern, in order to recognise the place, for it marks our half-way resting place.

And at last, at last, here is our house! The door is closed, all is silent and black. Our panels have been carefully shut by M. Sucre and Madame Prune; the rain streams down the wood of our old black walls.

In such weather it is impossible to allow Yves to return down hill, and wander along the shore in quest of a sampan. No, he shall not return on board to-night; we will put him up in our house His little room has indeed been already provided for in the conditions of our lease, and notwithstanding his discreet refusal, we immediately set to work to make it. Let us go in, take off our boots, shake ourselves like so many cats that have been out in a shower, and step up to our apartment.

In front of Buddha, the little lamps are burning; in the middle of the room, the night-blue gauze is stretched. On entering, the first impression is a favourable one; our dwelling is pretty, this evening, the late hour and deep silence give it an air of mystery. And then also, in such weather, it is always pleasant to get home.

Come, let us at once prepare Yves' room. Chrysanthème, quite elated at the prospect of having her big friend near her, sets to work with a good will; moreover, the task is an easy one, we have only to slip three or four paper panels in their grooves, to make at once a separate room or compartment in the great box we live in. I had thought that these panels were entirely white; but no! on each of them is a group of two storks painted in grey tints in those inevitable attitudes consecrated by Japanese art: one bearing aloft its proud head and haughtily raising its leg, the other scratching itself. Oh these storks! how sick one gets of them, at the end of a month spent in Japan!

Yves is now in bed and sleeping under our roof.

Sleep has come to him sooner than to me tonight; for somehow I fancy I had seen long glances exchanged between him and Chrysanthème.

I have left this little creature in his hands like a toy, and I begin to fear lest I should have thrown some perturbation in his mind. I do not trouble my head about this little Japanese girl. But Yves,—it would be decidedly wrong on his part, and would greatly diminish my faith in him.

We hear the rain falling on our old roof; the

cicalas are mute ; odours of wet earth reach us from the gardens and the mountain. I feel terribly dreary in this room to-night ; the noise of the little pipe irritates me more than usual, and as Chrysanthème crouches in front of her smoking-box, I suddenly discover in her an air of low breeding, in the very worst sense of the word.

I should hate her, my mousmé, if she were to entice Yves into committing a fault,—a fault which I should perhaps never be able to forgive.

XXX.

THE Y—— and Sikou-San couple were divorced yesterday. The Charles N—— and Campanule household is getting on very badly. They have had some annoyance with those prying, grinding, insupportable little men, dressed up in suits of grey, who are called police agents and who by threatening their landlord, has had them turned out of their house—(under the obsequious amiability of this people, there lurks a secret hatred towards us Europeans)—they are therefore obliged to accept their mother-in-law's hospitality, a very painful position. And

then Charles N—— fancies his wife is faithless.
It is hardly possible, however, for us to deceive
ourselves : these would-be maidens, to whom
M. Kangourou has introduced us, are young people who have already had in their lives one, or
perhaps more than one, adventure; it is therefore
only natural that we should have our suspicions.

The Z—— and Touki-San couple jog on,
quarrelling all the time.

My household maintains a more dignified air,
though it is none the less dreary.   I had indeed
thought of a divorce, but have really no good
reason for offering Chrysanthème such a
gratuitous affront ; moreover, there is another
more imperative reason why I should remain
quiet : I too have had difficulties with the
civilian authorities.

Day before yesterday, M. Sucre quite upset,
Madame Prune almost swooning, and Mdlle.
Oyouki bathed in tears, stormed my rooms. The
Niponese police agents had called and threatened
them with the law for letting rooms outside of
the European concession to a Frenchman mor-
ganatically married to a Japanese ; and the terror
of being prosecuted brought them to me, with a
thousand apologies, but the humble request
that I should leave.

The next day I therefore went off, accompanied by *the wonderfully tall friend*, who

expresses himself better than I do in Japanese, to the register office, with the full intention of making a terrible row.

In the language of this exquisitely polite people, terms of abuse are totally wanting; when very angry, one is obliged to be satisfied with using the *thou*, mark of *inferiority* and the *familiar conjugation*, habitual towards those of low birth. Seating myself on the table used for weddings, in the midst of all the flurried little policemen, I open the conversation in the following terms :

"In order that *thou shouldest* leave me in peace in the suburb I am inhabiting, what bribe must I offer *thee*, set of little beings more contemptible than any mere street porter ? "

Great and mute scandal, silent consternation, and low bows greet my words.

"Certainly," they at last reply, my honourable person shall not be molested, indeed they ask for nothing better. Only, in order to subscribe to the laws of the country, I ought to have come here and given my name and that of the young person that—with whom—

"Oh! that is going too far! I came here on purpose, contemptible creatures, not three weeks ago ! "

Then taking up myself the civil register, and turning over the pages rapidly, I found my signature and beside it the little hieroglyphics drawn by Chrysanthème :

" There, set of idiots, look at that ! "

Arrival of a very high functionary,—a ridiculous little old fellow in a black coat, who from his office has been listening to the row :

" What is the matter ? What is it ? What is this annoyance put upon the French officers ? "

I politely state my case to this personage, who cannot make apologies and promises enough. The little agents prostrate themselves on all fours, sink into the earth ; and we leave them, cold and dignified, without returning their bows.

M. Sucre and Madame Prune can now make their minds easy, they will not be disturbed again.

XXXI.

THE prolonged stay of the *Triomphante* in the dock, and the distance of our home from town, have been my pretext these last two or three days for not going up to Diou-djen-dji to see Chrysanthème.

It is dreary work though in these docks. With the early dawn a legion of little Japanese workmen invade us, bringing their dinners in baskets and gourds like the working-men in our arsenals, but with a needy, shabby appearance, and a ferreting, hurried manner which reminds one of rats. Silently they slip under the keel, at the bottom of the hold, in all the holes, sawing, nailing, repairing.

The heat is intense in this spot, overshadowed by the rocks and tangled masses of foliage.

At two o'clock, in the broad sunlight, we have a new and far prettier kind of invasion: that of the beetles and butterflies.

Butterflies as wonderful as those on the fans. Some all black, giddily dash up against us, so light and airy that they seem merely a pair of quivering wings fastened together without any body.

Yves astonished, gazes at them, saying in his boyish manner: "Oh, I saw such a big one just now, such a big one, it quite frightened me; I thought it was a bat attacking me."

A steersman who has captured a very curious specimen, carries it off carefully to press between the leaves of his signal-book, like a flower. Another sailor passing by, taking his small roast to the oven in a mess-bowl, looks at him funnily and says:

"You had much better give it to me. I'd cook it!"

XXXII.

IT is nearly five days since I have abandoned my home and Chrysanthème.

Since yesterday we have had a storm of rain and wind—(a typhoon that has passed or is passing over us). We beat to quarters in the middle of the night to *lower the top-masts, strike the lower yards,* and take every precaution against bad weather. The butterflies no longer hover around us, but everything tosses and writhes overhead : on the steep slopes of the mountain, the trees shiver, the long grasses bend low as though in pain ; terrible gusts rack them with a hissing sound ; branches, bamboo leaves, and earth are showered down like rain upon us.

In this land of pretty little trifles, this violent

tempest is out of all harmony; it seems as if
its efforts were exaggerated and its music too
loud.

Towards evening the big dark clouds roll by
so rapidly, that the showers are of short duration and soon pass over. Then I attempt a
walk on the mountain above us, in the wet
verdure: little pathways lead up it, between
thickets of camelias and bamboos.

Waiting till a shower is over, I take refuge
in the courtyard of an old temple half-way up
the hill, buried in a wood of centennial trees of
gigantic branches; it is reached by granite steps,
through strange gateways, as deeply furrowed
as the old Celtic dolmens. The trees have also
invaded this yard; the daylight is overcast
with a greenish tint, and the drenching rain
that pours down in torrents, is full of torn-up
leaves and moss. Old granite monsters, of
unknown shapes, are seated in the corners, and
grimace with smiling ferocity; their faces are
full of indefinable mystery that makes me
shudder amid the moaning music of the wind,
in the gloomy shadows of the clouds and
branches.

They could not have resembled the Japanese
of our day, the men who had thus conceived

these ancient temples, who built them everywhere, and filled the country with them, even in its most solitary nooks.

An hour later, in the twilight of that stormy day, on the same mountain, I chanced upon a clump of trees somewhat similar to oaks in appearance; they, too, have been twisted by the tempest, and the tufts of undulating grass at their feet are laid low, tossed about in every direction. There, I suddenly have brought back to my mind, my first impression of a strong wind in the woods of Limoise, in the province of Saintonge, some twenty-eight years ago, in a month of March of my childhood.

That, the first storm of wind my eyes ever beheld sweeping over the landscape, blew in just the opposite quarter of the world,—and many years have rapidly passed over that memory,—since then the best part of my life has been spent.

I refer too often, I fancy, to my childhood; I am foolishly fond of it. But it seems to me that then only did I truly experience sensations or impressions; the smallest trifles I then saw or heard were full of deep and hidden meaning, recalling past images out of oblivion, and re-awakening memories of prior existences; or else they were presentiments of existences to come, future incarnations in the land of dreams, expectations of wondrous marvels that life and the world held in store for me,—for later, no doubt, when I should be grown up.   Well, I have grown up, and have found nothing that answered to my undefinable expectations ; on the contrary, all has narrowed and darkened around me, my vague recollections of the past have become blurred, the horizons before me have slowly closed in and become full of a grey darkness.   Soon will my time come to return to eternal rest, and I shall leave this world without having understood the mysterious wherefore of these mirages of my childhood ; I shall bear away with me a lingering regret, of I know not what lost home that I have failed to find, of the unknown beings ardently longed for, whom, alas, I have never embraced.

Rossi

XXXIII.

WITH many affectations, M. Sucre has dipped the tip of his delicate paint-brush in Indian ink and traced a couple of charming storks on a pretty sheet of rice-paper, offering them to me in the most gracious manner, as a souvenir of himself. They are here, in my cabin on board, and whenever I look at them, I can fancy I see M. Sucre tracing them in an airy manner, with elegant facility.

The saucer in which M. Sucre mixes his ink, is in itself a little gem. Chiselled out of a piece of jade, it represents a tiny lake with a carved border imitating rockwork. On this border is a little mama toad, also in jade, advancing as though to bathe in the little lake in which M. Sucre carefully keeps a few drops of very dark liquid. The mama toad has four

little baby toads, equally in jade, one perched on her head, the other three playing about under her.

M. Sucre has painted many a stork in the course of his lifetime, and he really excels in reproducing groups and duets, if one may so express it, of this kind of bird. Few Japanese possess the art of interpreting this subject in a manner at once so rapid and so tasteful ; first he draws the two beaks, then the four claws, then the backs, the feathers, dash, dash, dash,— with a dozen strokes of his clever brush, held in his daintily posed hand, it is done, and always perfectly well done !

M. Kangourou relates, without seeing anything wrong in it whatever, that formerly this talent was of great service to M. Sucre. It appears that Madame Prune,—how shall I say such a thing, and who could guess it now, on beholding so devout and sedate an old lady, with eyebrows

so scrupulously shaven!—however, it appears that Madame Prune used to receive a great many visits from gentlemen,—gentlemen who always came alone, and it led to some gossip. Therefore, when Madame Prune was engaged

with one visitor, if a new arrival made his
appearance, the ingenious husband, to make
him wait patiently, and to while away the
time in the ante-room, immediately offered to
paint him some storks in a variety of attitudes.

And this is how, in Nagasaki, all the
Japanese gentlemen of a certain age, have in
their collections two or three of these little pictures, for which they are indebted to the delicate
and original talent of M. Sucre.

XXXIV.

AT about six o'clock, while I was on duty, the *Triomphante* left her prison walls between the mountains and came out of dock. After a great uproar of manœuvring we took up our old moorings in the roadstead, at the foot of the Dioudjen-dji hills. The weather was again calm and cloudless, the sky presenting a peculiar clearness as though it had been swept clean by the cyclone, an exceeding transparency bringing out the minutest details of the far distance till then unseen; as if the terrible blast had blown away every vestige of the floating mists and left behind it nothing but void and boundless space. The colouring of woods and mountains stood out again in the resplendent verdancy of spring after the torrents of rain, like the wet colours of some freshly washed painting. The sampans and junks, which for the last three days had been lying under shelter, had now put out to sea, and the bay was covered with their white sails, which looked like an immense flight of seabirds.

At eight o'clock, at nightfall, our manœuvre being at an end, I embarked with Yves on board a sampan; this time it is he who is carrying me off and taking me back to my home.

On land, a delicious perfume of new-mown hay greets us, and the road across the mountains lies bathed in glorious moonlight. We go straight up to Diou-djen-dji to join Chrysanthème; I feel almost remorseful, although I hardly show it, for my neglect of her.

Looking up, I recognise from afar my little house, perched on high. It is wide open and lit up; I even hear the sound of a guitar. Then I perceive the gilt head of my Buddha between the little bright flames of its two hanging night-lamps. Now Chrysanthème appears on the verandah, looking out as if she expected us; and with her wonderful bows of hair and long falling sleeves, her silhouette is thoroughly Niponese.

As I enter, she comes forward to kiss me, in a graceful, though rather hesitating manner, while Oyouki, more demonstrative, throws her arms around me.

It is with a certain pleasure that I see once more this Japanese home, which I wonder to find still mine when I had almost forgotten its existence. Chrysanthème has put fresh flowers in our vases, spread out her hair, donned her best clothes, and lighted our lamps to honour my return. From the balcony she had watched the *Triomphante* leave the dock, and, in the expectation of our now prompt return, she had made her preparations; then, to while away the time, she was studying a duet on the guitar with Oyouki. Not a question or reproach did she make. On the contrary:

"We quite understood," she said, "how impossible it was, in such dreadful weather, to undertake so lengthy a crossing in a sampan."

She smiled like a pleased child, and I should be fastidious indeed if I did not admit that to-night she is charming.

I announce my intention of starting off for a long stroll through Nagasaki; we will take Oyouki-San and two little cousins who happen to be here, as well as some other neighbours, if they wish it ; we will buy the funniest toys, eat all sorts of cakes, and amuse ourselves to our hearts' content.

"How lucky we are to be here, just at the right moment," they exclaim, jumping with joy. "How fortunate we are ! This very evening  there is to be a pilgrim-mage to the great temple of the *Jumping Tortoise!* The whole town will be there ; all our married friends have already started, the whole set, X——, Y——, Z——, Touki-San, Campanule, and Jonquille, with *the friend of amazing height*.   And these two, poor Chrysanthème and poor Oyouki, would have been obliged to stay at home with heavy hearts, because we had not yet arrived, and because Madame Prune had been seized with faintness and hysterics after her dinner.

Quickly the mousmés must deck themselves out.   Chrysanthème is ready ; Oyouki hurries, changes her dress, and, putting on a mouse-coloured grey robe, begs me to arrange the bows of her fine sash—black satin lined with

yellow—sticking at the same time in her hair a
silver top-knot. We light our lanterns, swing-

ing at the end of little sticks ; M. Sucre, overwhelming us with thanks for his daughter,
accompanies us on all fours to the door,—and

we go off gaily through the clear and balmy night.

Below, we find the town in all the animation of a great holiday. The streets are thronged ; the crowd passes by,—a laughing, capricious, slow, unequal tide, flowing onwards, however, steadily in the same direction, towards the same goal. There arises therefrom an immense but light murmur in which dominate the sounds of laughter, and the low-toned interchange of polite speeches. Then follow lanterns upon lanterns. Never in my life have I seen so many, so variegated, so complicated, and so extraordinary.

We follow, drifting with the surging crowd, borne along by it. There are groups of women of every age, decked out in their smartest clothes, crowds of mousmés with aigrettes of flowers in their hair, or little silver top-knots like Oyouki,—pretty little physiognomies, little narrow eyes peeping between slit lids like those of a new-born kitten, fat pale little cheeks, round, puffed-out, half-opened lips. They are pretty, nevertheless, these little Niponese, in their smiles and childishness.

The men, on the other hand, wear many a pot hat, pompously added to the long national robe, and giving thereby a finishing touch to their cheerful ugliness, resembling nothing so much as dancing monkeys. They carry boughs in their hands, whole shrubs even, amidst the foliage of which dangle all sorts of curious lanterns in the shape of imps and birds.

As we advance in the direction of the temple, the streets become more noisy and crowded. All along the houses are endless stalls raised on trestles, displaying sweetmeats of every colour, toys, branches of flowers, nosegays, and masks. There are masks everywhere, boxes full of them, carts full of them; the most popular being the one that represents the livid and cunning muzzle, contracted as by a death-like grimace, the long straight ears, sharp-pointed teeth of the white fox, sacred to the God of Rice. There are also others symbolic of gods or monsters, livid, grimacing, convulsed, with wigs and beards of natural hair. All manner of folk, even children, purchase these horrors, and fasten them over their faces Every sort of instrument is for sale, amongst them many of those crystal trumpets which sound so strangely,—this evening they are enormous, six feet long at least,—and the noise they make is unlike anything ever heard before : one would say gigantic turkeys gobbling amongst the crowd, and striving to inspire fear.

In the religious amusements of this people
it is not possible for us to penetrate the mys-
teriously hidden meaning of things ; we cannot
divine the boundary at which jesting stops and
mystic fear steps in. These customs, these symbols, these masks, all that
tradition and atavism
have jumbled together in
the Japanese brain, pro-
ceed from sources utterly
dark and unknown to
us ; even the oldest re-
cords fail to explain them
to us in anything but a
superficial and cursory

manner, *simply because we have absolutely
nothing in common with this people.* We pass
in the midst of their mirth and their laughter
without understanding the wherefore, so totally
does it differ from our own.

Chrysanthème with Yves, Oyouki with me,
Fraise and Zinia, our cousins, walking
before us under our watchful eye, slowly move
through the crowd, holding each others' hands
lest we should lose one another.

All along the streets leading to the temple,

the wealthy inhabitants have decorated the fronts
of their houses with a quantity of vases and
nosegays. The peculiar shed-like buildings

habitual in this country, with their open plat-
form frontage, are particularly well suited for
the display of choice objects; all the houses
have been thrown open, and the interiors are
hung with draperies that hide the back of the

apartments. In front of these hangings and slightly standing back from the movement of the passing crowd, the various exhibited articles are methodically placed in a row, under the full glare of hanging lamps. Hardly any flowers compose the nosegays, nothing but foliage,—some rare and priceless, others chosen as if purposely from amongst the commonest plants, arranged however with such taste as to make them appear new and choice ; ordinary lettuce leaves, tall cabbage stalks are placed with exquisite artificial taste in vessels of marvellous workmanship. All the vases are of bronze, but the designs are varied according to each changing fancy : some complicated and twisted ; others, and by far the largest number, graceful and simple, but of a simplicity so studied and exquisite that to our eyes they seem the revelation of an unknown art, the subversion of all acquired notions on form.

On turning a corner of a street, by good luck we meet our married comrades of the *Triomphante* and Jonquille, Touki-San and Campanule ! Bows and curtsies are exchanged by the mousmés, reciprocal manifestations of joy at meeting ; then, forming a compact band, we are carried off by the ever-increasing crowd and continue our progress in the direction of the temple.

The streets gradually ascend (the temples are always built on a height) ; and by degrees as we mount up, there is added to the brilliant fairyland of lanterns and costumes, yet another, ethereally blue in the haze of distance ; all Nagasaki, its pagodas, its mountains, its still waters full of the rays of moonlight, seem to rise up with us into the air. Slowly, step by step, one may say it springs up around, enveloping in one great shimmering veil all the foreground, with its dazzling red lights and many-coloured streamers.

No doubt we are getting near, for here are the religious steps, porticos and monsters hewn out of enormous blocks of granite. We now have to climb a series of steps, almost carried by the surging crowd ascending with us.

The temple court-yard ; we have arrived.

This is the last and most astonishing scene in the evening's fairy-tale,—a luminous and weird scene with fantastic distances lighted up by the

moon and the gigantic trees, the sacred crypto-
merias, stretching forth their dark sombre boughs
like a vast dome.

Here we are all seated with our mousmés,
beneath the light awning wreathed in flowers,
of one of the many little tea-houses improvised

in this courtyard. We
are on a terrace at the
top of the great steps,
up which the crowd con-
tinues to flock ; we are
at the foot of a portico
which stands up erect
with the rigid massive-
ness of a colossus against
the dark night sky; at the
foot also of a monster,

who stares down upon us, with his big stony
eyes, his cruel grimace and smile.

This portico and the monster are the two
great overwhelming masses in the foreground
of the incredible scene before us ; they stand
out with dazzling boldness against the vague
and ashy blue of the distant sphere beyond ;
behind them, Nagasaki is spread out in a bird's-
eye view, faintly outlined in the transparent
darkness with myriads of little coloured lights,
and the extravagantly dented profile of the

mountains is delineated on the starlit sky, blue
upon blue, transparency upon transparency.   A
corner of the harbour is also visible, high up,

undefined like a lake lost in the clouds; the
water faintly illumined by a ray of moonlight
shining forth like a sheet of silver.

Around us the long crystal trumpets keep up

their gobble. Groups of polite and frivolous
persons pass and repass like fantastic shadows;
childish bands of small-eyed mousmés with
smile so candidly meaningless and chignons
shining through their bright silver flowers;
ugly men waving at the end of long branches
their eternal lanterns shaped like birds, gods or
insects.

Behind us, in the lit-up and wide-open
temple, the bonzes sit, immovable embodiments
of doctrine, in the glittering sanctuary inhabited
by divinities, chimeras and symbols. The
crowd, monotonously droning its mingled prayers
and laughter, presses around them, sowing its
alms broadcast; with a continuous jingle, the
money rolls on the ground into the precincts
reserved to the priests, where the white mats
entirely disappear under the mass of many-
sized coins accumulated there as after a deluge
of silver and bronze.

We, however, feel thoroughly at sea in the
midst of this festivity; we look on, we laugh
like the rest, we make foolish and senseless
remarks in a language insufficiently learned,
and which this evening, I know not why, we
can hardly understand. Notwithstanding the
night breeze, we find it very hot under our
awning, and we absorb quantities of funny-

looking water-ices, served in cups, which taste like scented frost, or rather like flowers steeped in snow. Our mousmés order for themselves great bowls of candied beans mixed with hail,—real hail-stones such as we would pick up after a hail-storm in March.

Glou! glou! glou! the crystal trumpets slowly repeat their notes, the powerful sonority of which has a laboured and smothered sound, as though they came from under water; they mingle with the jingling of rattles and the noise of castanets. We also have the impression of being carried away in the irresistible swing of this incomprehensible gaiety, composed in proportions we can scarcely measure, of elements mystic, puerile and even ghastly. A sort of religious terror is diffused by the hidden idols divined in the temple behind us; by the mumbled prayers, confusedly heard; above all, by the horrible heads in lacquered wood, representing foxes, which, as they pass, hide human faces,—hideous livid masks.

In the gardens and outbuildings of the temple the most inconceivable mountebanks have taken up their quarters, their black streamers, painted with white letters, looking like funereal trappings as they float in the wind from the top of their tall flagstaffs. Hither we turn our steps, as soon as our mousmés have ended their orisons and bestowed their alms.

In one of the booths a man stretched on a table, flat on his back, is alone on the stage ; puppets of almost human size, with horribly grinning masks, spring out of his body ; they

speak, gesticulate, then fall back like empty rags ; with a sudden spring they start up again, change their costumes, change their faces, tearing about in one continual frenzy. Suddenly three, even four appear at the same time ; they are nothing more than the four limbs of the outstretched man, whose legs and arms, raised on high, are each one dressed up, and capped with a wig under which peers a mask ; between these phantoms tremendous fighting and battling take place, and many a sword-thrust is exchanged. The most fearful of all is a certain puppet representing an old hag ; every time she appears, with her weird head and ghastly grin, the lights burn low, the

music of the accompanying orchestra moans forth
a sinister strain given by the flutes, mingled with
a rattling tremolo which sounds like the clatter

of bones. This creature evidently plays an
ugly part in the piece,—that of a horrible old
ghoul, spiteful and famished. Still more appalling than her person is her shadow, which, pro-

jected upon a white screen, is abnormally and vividly distinct; by means of some unknown process this shadow, which nevertheless follows all her movements, assumes the aspect of a wolf. At a given moment the hag turns round and presents the profile of her distorted snub nose as she accepts the bowl of rice which is offered to her; on the screen at the very same instant appears the elongated outline of the wolf, with its pointed ears, its muzzle and chops, its great teeth and hanging tongue. The orchestra grinds, wails, quivers; then suddenly bursts out into funereal shrieks, like a concert of owls; the hag is now eating, and her wolfish shadow is eating also, greedily moving its jaws and nibbling at another shadow easy to recognize,—the arm of a little child.

We now go on to see the *great salamander* of Japan, an animal rare in this country, and quite unknown elsewhere, a great cold mass, sluggish and benumbed, looking like some antediluvian *experiment*, forgotten in the inner seas of this archipelago.

Next comes the trained elephant, the terror of our mousmés, the equilibrists, the menagerie.

It is one o'clock in the morning before we are back at Diou-djen-dji.

We first get Yves to bed in the little paper room he has already once occupied. Then we go to bed ourselves, after the inevitable preparations, the smoking of the little pipe, and the *pan! pan! pan! pan!* on the edge of the box.

Suddenly Yves begins to move restlessly in his sleep, to toss about, giving great kicks on the wall, and making a frightful noise.

What can be the matter? I at once imagine that he must be dreaming of the old hag and her wolfish shadow. Chrysanthème raises herself on her elbow and listens, with astonishment depicted on her face.

Ah! happy thought! she has discovered what is tormenting him:

" Ka!" (mosquitoes) she says.

And, to impress the more forcibly her meaning on my mind, she pinches my arm so hard with her little pointed nails, at the same time imitating, with such an amusing play of her features, the grimace of a person who is stung, that I exclaim—

" Oh! stop, Chrysanthème, this pantomime is too expressive, and indeed useless! I know the word *Ka*, and had quite understood, I assure you."

It is done so drolly and so quickly, with such

a pretty pout, that in truth I cannot think of
being angry, although I shall certainly have
to-morrow a blue mark on my arm ; about that
there is no doubt.

"Come, we must get up and go to Yves'
rescue; he cannot be allowed to go on thumping
in that manner.   Let us take a lantern, and see
what has happened."

It was indeed the mosquitoes.   They are
hovering in a thick cloud about him ; those of
the house and those of the garden all seem collected together, swarming and buzzing.   Chrysanthème indignantly burns several at the flame
of her lantern, and shows me others : "Hou!"
covering the white paper walls.

He, tired out with his day's amusement, sleeps
on ; but his slumbers are restless, as can be
easily imagined.   Chrysanthème gives him a
shake, wishing him to get up and share our blue
mosquito net.

After a little pressing he does as he is bid
and follows us, looking like an overgrown boy
only half awake.   I make no objection to this
singular hospitality ; after all, it looks so little
like a bed, the matting we are to share, and
we sleep in our clothes, as we always do according to the Niponese fashion.   After all, on a
journey in a railway, do not the most estimable

ladies stretch themselves witnout demur oy the side of gentlemen unknown to them ?

I have however placed Chrysanthème's little wooden block in the centre of the gauze tent, between our two pillows.

Then, without saying a word, in a dignified manner as though she were rectifying an error of etiquette that I had inadvertently committed, Chrysanthème takes up her piece of wood, putting in its place my snake-skin drum; I shall therefore be in the middle between the two. It is really more correct, decidedly much more proper; Chrysanthème is evidently a very decorous young person.

Returning on board next morning, in the clear morning sun, we walk through pathways full of dew; accompanied by a band of funny little mousmés of six or eight years of age, who are going off to school.

Needless to say that the cicalas around us keep up their perpetual sonorous chirping. The mountain smells delicious. The atmosphere, the dawning day, the infantine grace of these little girls in their long frocks and shiny chignons, all is redundant with freshness and youth. The flowers and grasses on which we tread sparkle with dewdrops, exhaling a perfume of freshness. What undying beauty there is, even in Japan, in the first fresh morning hours in the country, and the dawning hours of life !

Besides, I am quite ready to admit the attractiveness of the little Japanese children ; some of them are most fascinating. But how is it that their charm vanishes so rapidly and is so quickly replaced by the elderly grimace, the smiling ugliness, the monkeyish face ?

Rossi

XXXV.

My mother-in-law Madame Renoncule's small garden is, without exception, one of the most melancholy spots I have seen during all my peregrinations through the world.

Oh, the slow, enervating, dull hours spent in idle and diffuse conversation in the dimly lighted verandah! Oh, the horrid peppered jam in the microscopic pots! In the middle of the town, enclosed by four walls, is this park of five yards square, with little lakes, little

mountains, and little rocks, where all wears
an antiquated appearance, and everything is
covered with a greenish mouldiness from want
of sun.

Nevertheless a true feeling for nature has
inspired this tiny representation of a wild spot.
The rocks are well placed, the dwarf cedars,

no taller than cabbages,
stretch their gnarled
boughs over the valleys
in the attitude of giants
wearied by the weight
of centuries ; and their
look of *big trees* per-
plexes one and falsifies
the perspective. When
from the dark recesses
of the apartment one
perceives at a certain distance this diminutive
landscape dimly lighted up, the wonder is
whether it is all artificial, or whether one is not
oneself the victim of some morbid illusion ; and
if it is not indeed a real country view seen
through a distorted vision out of focus, or through
the wrong end of a telescope.

To any one familiar with Japanese life my
mother-in-law's house in itself reveals a refined
nature,—complete nudity, two or three screens

placed here and there, a teapot, a vase full of lotus-flowers, and nothing more. Woodwork devoid of paint or varnish, but carved in most

elaborate and capricious openwork, the whiteness of the pinewood being kept up by constant scrubbings of soap and water. The posts and beams of the framework are varied by the most fanciful taste: some are cut in precise geometrical forms ; others artificially twisted, imitating trunks of old trees covered with tropical creepers. Everywhere little hiding - places, little nooks, little closets concealed in the most ingenious and unexpected manner under the immaculate uniformity of the white paper panels.

I cannot help smiling when I think of some of the so-called *Japanese* drawing-rooms, over-crowded with knick-knacks and curios and hung with coarse gold embroideries on exported satins, of our Parisian fine ladies. I would advise those persons to come and look at the houses of people of taste out here ; to visit the white solitudes of the palaces at Yeddo. In France we have works of art in order to enjoy them ; here they possess them merely to ticket them and lock them up carefully in a kind of mysterious underground room shut in by iron gratings called a *godoun*. On rare occasions, only to honour some visitor of distinction, do they open this impenetrable depositary. The true Japanese manner of understanding luxury consists in a scrupulous and indeed almost excessive cleanliness, white mats and white woodwork ; an appearance of extreme simplicity, and an incredible nicety in the most infinitesimal details.

My mother-in-law seems to be really a very nice woman, and were it not for the insurmountable feeling of spleen the sight of her garden produces on me, I would often go and see her.   She has nothing in common with the mammas of Jonquille, Campanule or Touki : she is vastly their superior ; and then I can see that she has been very good-looking and stylish. Her past life puzzles me ; but in my position as a son-in-law, good manners prevent my making further enquiries.

Some assert that she was formerly a celebrated guécha in Yeddo, who lost public favour by her folly in becoming a mother.   This would account for her daughter's talent on the guitar ; she had probably herself taught her the touch and style of the Conservatory.

Since the birth of Chrysanthème (her eldest child and first cause of this loss of favour), my mother-in-law, an expansive although distinguished nature, has fallen seven times into the same fatal error, and I have two little sisters-in-law: Mdlle. La Neige,* and Mdlle. La Lune,† as well as five little brothers-in-law : Cerisier, Pigeon, Liseron, Or, and Bambou.

* In Japanese : *Oyouki-San* (like Madame Prune's daughter).
† In Japanese : *Tsouki-San.*

Little Bambou is four years old,—a yellow
baby, fat and round all over, with fine bright
eyes; coaxing and jolly, sleeping whenever he
is not laughing. Of all my Niponese family,
Bambou is the one I love the most.

XXXVI.

WE have spent the day,—Yves, Chrysanthème, Oyouki and myself, — wandering
through dark and dusty nooks, dragged hither
and thither by four quick-footed djins, in search
of antiquities in the bric-à-brac shops.

Towards sunset, Chrysanthème, who has
wearied me more than ever since the morning,
and who doubtless has perceived it, pulls a very
long face, declares herself ill, and begs leave
to spend the night at her mother's, Madame
Renoncule.

I agree to this with the best grace in the
world ; let her go, tiresome little mousmé !
Oyouki will carry a message to her parents, who

will shut up our rooms ; we shall spend the
evening, Yves and I, in roaming about as fancy
takes us, without any mousmé dragging at our
heels, and shall afterwards regain our own
quarters on board the *Triomphante*, without
having the trouble of climbing up that hill.

First of all, we make an attempt to dine
together in some fashionable tea-house. Impossible, there is not a place to be had ; all
the absurd paper rooms, all the compartments
contrived by so many ingenious dodges of
slipping and sliding panels, all the nooks and
corners in the little gardens are filled with
Japanese men and women eating impossible
and incredible little dishes ! numberless young
dandies are dining *tête-à-tête* with the lady of
their choice, and sounds of dancing girls and
music issue from the private rooms.

The fact is, that to-day is the third and last
day of the great pilgrimage to the temple of the
Jumping Tortoise, of which we saw the com-
mencement yesterday, and all Nagasaki is at
this time given over to amusement.

At the tea-house of the *Indescribable Butterflies*, which is also full to overflowing, but where
we are well-known, they have had the bright
idea of throwing a temporary flooring over the
little lake,—the pond where the gold-fish live,

and it is here that our meal is served, in the pleasant freshness of the fountain which continues its murmur under our feet.

After dinner, we follow the faithful and ascend again to the temple.

Up there we find the same elfin revelry, the same masks, the same music. We seat ourselves, as before, under a gauze tent and sip odd little drinks tasting of flowers. But this evening we are alone, and the absence of the band of mousmés, whose familiar little faces formed a bond of union between this holiday-making people and ourselves, separates and isolates us more than usual from the profusion of oddities in the midst of which we seem to be lost. Beneath us, lies always the immense blue background : Nagasaki illumined by moonlight, and the expanse of silvered, glittering water, which seems like a vaporous vision suspended in mid-air. Behind us is the great open temple, where the bonzes officiate to the accompaniment of sacred bells and wooden clappers,—looking, from where we sit, more like puppets than anything else, some squatting in rows like peaceful mummies, others executing rhythmical marches before the golden background where stand the gods. We do not laugh to-night, and speak but little, more forcibly struck by the scene than we were on the first night ; we only look on, trying to understand. Suddenly, Yves turning round, says :

" Hullo ! brother, your mousmé ! ! "

Actually there she is, behind him ; Chrysanthème almost on all fours, hidden between the paws of a great granite beast, half tiger, half dog, against which our fragile tent is leaning.

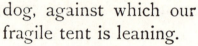

" She pulled my trousers with her nails, for all the world like a little cat," said Yves, still full of surprise, " positively like a cat ! "

She remains bent double in the most humble form of salutation; she smiles timidly, afraid of being ill received, and the head of my little brother-in-law, Bambou, appears smiling too, just above her own. She has brought this little *mousko* * with her, perched astride on her back ; he looks as absurd as ever, with his shaven head, his long frock and the great bows of his silken sash. There they both stand gazing at us, anxious to know how their joke will be taken.

For my part, I have not the least idea of giving them a cold reception ; on the contrary,

---

* *Mousko* is the masculine of *mousmé*, and signifies little boy. Excessive politeness makes it *mousko-san* (Mr. little boy).

the meeting amuses me. It even strikes me
that it is rather pretty of Chrysanthème to
come round in this way, and to bring Bambou-
San to the festival; though it savours somewhat of her low breeding, to tell the truth, to

have tacked him on to her back, as the poorer
Japanese women do with their little ones

However, let her sit down between Yves and
myself : and let them bring her those iced beans
she loves so much ; and we will take the jolly
little *mousko* on our knees and cram him with
sugar and sweetmeats to his heart's content.

The evening over, when we begin to think of

leaving, and of going down again, Chrysanthème replaces her little Bambou astride upon
her back, and sets forth, bending forward under
his weight and painfully dragging her Cinde-
rella slippers over the granite steps and flag-
stones.   Yes, decidedly low this conduct! but
low in the best sense of the word : nothing in it
displeases me ; I even consider Chrysanthème's
affection for Bambou-San engaging and attractive in its simplicity.

One cannot deny this merit to the Japanese,
—a great love for little children, and a talent for
amusing them, for making them laugh, invent-
ing comical toys for them, making the morning
of their life happy ; for a speciality in dressing
them, arranging their heads, and giving to the
whole little personage the most diverting appearance possible.   It is the only thing I really
like about this country : the babies and the
manner in which they are understood.

On our way we meet our married friends of
the *Triomphante*, who, much surprised at seeing
me with this *mousko*, chaffingly exclaim :

" What ! a son already ? "

Down in the town, we make a point of bid-
ding goodbye to Chrysanthème at the turning
of the street where her mother lives. She smiles
undecided, declares herself well again, and begs

to return to our house on the heights. This did not precisely enter into my plans, I confess. However, it would look very ungracious to refuse.

So be it! But we must carry the *mousko* home to his mamma, and then begin, by the flickering light of a new lantern bought afresh from Madame Très-Propre, our weary homeward ascent.

Here, however, we find ourselves in another predicament: this ridiculous little Bambou insists upon coming with us! No, he will take no denial, we must take him with us. This is out of all reason, quite impossible!

However, it will not do to make him cry, on the night of a great festival too, poor little *mousko*. So we must send a message to Madame Renoncule, that she may not be uneasy about him, and as there will soon not be a living creature on the footpaths of Diou-djen-dji to laugh at us, we will take it in turn, Yves and I, to carry him on our back, all the way up that climb in the darkness.

And here am I, who did not wish to return this way to-night, dragging a mousmé by the hand, actually carrying an extra burden in the shape of a *mousko* on my back. What an irony of fate!

As I had expected, all our shutters and doors are closed, bolted and barred; no one expects us, and we have to make a prodigious noise at the door.   Chrysanthème sets to work and calls with all her might :

"Ho! Oumé-San-an-an-an!"   (In English: "Hi! Madame Pru-u-u-u-une!")

These intonations in her little voice are unknown to me ; her long-drawn call in the echoing darkness of midnight has so strange an accent, something so unexpected and wild, that it impresses me with a dismal feeling of far-off exile.

At last Madame Prune appears to open the door to us, only half awake and much astonished; by way of a night-cap she wears a monstrous

cotton turban, on the blue ground of which a few white storks are playfully disporting themselves. Holding in the tips of her fingers with an affectation of graceful fright, the long stalk of her beflowered lantern, she gazes intently into our faces, one after another, to assure herself of our identity; but the poor old lady cannot get over the *mousko* I am carrying.

XXXVII.

At first it was only to Chrysanthème's guitar that I listened with pleasure : now I am beginning to like her singing also.

She has nothing of the theatrical, or the deep assumed voice of the virtuoso ; on the contrary, her notes, always very high, are soft, thin, and plaintive.

She will often teach Oyouki some romance, slow and dreamy, which she has composed, or which comes back to her mind. Then they both astonish me, for on their well-tuned guitars they will search out accompaniments in parts, and try again each time that the chords are not perfectly true to their ear, without ever losing themselves in the confusion of these dissonant harmonies, always weird and always melancholy.

Generally, while their music is going on, I am writing in the verandah, with the superb panorama stretched out in front of me. I write, seated on a mat on the floor and leaning upon a little Japanese desk, ornamented with swallows in relief; my ink is Chinese, my ink-stand, just like that of my landlord, is in jade, with dear little frogs and toads carved on the rim. In short, I am writing my memoirs,—exactly as M. Sucre does downstairs! Occasionally I fancy I resemble him—a very disagreeable fancy.

My memoirs,—composed of incongruous details, minute observations of colours, shapes, scents, and sounds.

It is true that a complete imbroglio, worthy of a romance, seems ever threatening to appear upon my monotonous horizon; a regular intrigue seems ever ready to explode in the midst of this little world of mousmés and grasshoppers: Chrysanthème in love with Yves; Yves with Chrysanthème; Oyouki with me; I with no one. We might even find here, ready to hand, the elements of a fratricidal drama, were we in any other country than Japan; but we are in Japan, and under the narrowing and dwarfing influence of the surroundings, which turn everything into ridicule, nothing will come of it all.

XXXVIII.

THERE is, in this good town of Nagasaki, towards five or six o'clock in the evening, one hour of the day more comical than any other. At this moment every living being is naked: children, young people, old people, old men, old women, every one is seated in a tub of some sort, taking a bath. This takes place no matter where, without the slightest screen, in the gardens, the courtyards, in the shops, even upon the thresholds, in order to give greater facility for conversation among the neighbours from one side of the street to the other. In this situation visitors are received; and the bather, without any hesitation, leaves his tub, holding in his hand his little towel (invariably blue), to offer the caller a seat, and to exchange with him some amiable remarks. Nevertheless, neither the mousmés nor the old ladies gain anything by appearing in this primæval costume. A Japanese woman, deprived of her long dress and her huge sash with its pretentious bows, is nothing but a diminutive yellow being, with crooked legs and flat, unshapely bust; she has no longer a remnant of her artificial little charms, which have completely disappeared in company with her costume.

There is yet another hour, at once joyous and melancholy, a little later when twilight falls, when the sky seems one vast veil of yellow, against which stand the clear-cut outlines of jagged mountains and lofty, fantastic pagodas. It is the hour at which, in the labyrinth of little grey streets down below, the sacred lamps begin to twinkle in the ever-open houses, in front of the ancestors' altars and the familiar Buddhas; while outside, darkness creeps over all, and the thousand and one indentations and peaks of the old roofs are depicted, as if in black festoons, on the clear golden sky. At this moment, there suddenly passes over merry, laughing Japan a sombre shadow, strange, weird, a breath of antiquity, of savagery, of something indefinable, which casts a gloom of sadness. And then the only gaiety that remains is the gaiety of the population of young children, of little mouskos and little mousmés, who spread themselves like a wave through the streets filled with shadow, as they swarm out from schools and workshops. On the dark background of all these wooden buildings, the little blue and scarlet dresses stand out in startling contrast,—drolly bedizened, drolly draped ; and the fine loops of the sashes, the flowers, the silver or gold top-knots stuck in these baby chignons, add to the vivid effect.

They amuse themselves, they chase each other, their great pagoda sleeves fly widely open, and these tiny little mousmés of ten, of five years old, or even younger still, have lofty head-dresses and imposing bows of hair arranged on their little heads, like grown-up women. Oh ! what loves of supremely absurd dolls at this hour of twilight gambol through the streets, in their long frocks, blowing their crystal trumpets, or running with all their might to start their fanciful kites. This juvenile world of Japan—ludicrous by birth, and fated to

become more so as the years roll on—starts in life with singular amusements, with strange cries and shouts; its playthings are somewhat ghastly, and would frighten the children of other countries; even the kites have great squinting eyes and vampire shapes.

And every evening, in the little dark streets. bursts forth this overflow of joyousness, fresh. childish, but withal grotesque to excess. It would be difficult to have any idea of the incredible things which, carried by the wind, float in the evening air.

XXXIX.

LITTLE Chrysanthème is always arrayed in
dark colours, a sign here of aristocratic distinction.   While her friends Oyouki-San, Madame
Touki and others delight in loud-striped stuffs,
and stick gorgeous ornaments in their chignons,
she always wears navy-blue or neutral grey,
fastened round her waist with great black sashes
brocaded in tender shades, and puts nothing in
her hair but amber-coloured tortoise-shell pins.
If she were of noble descent she would wear
embroidered on her dress in the middle of the
back a little white circle looking like a post-
mark with some design in the centre of it—the
leaf of a tree generally ; and this would be her
coat of arms.   There is really nothing wanting
but this little heraldic blazon on the back to

give her the appearance of a lady of the highest position.

In Japan the smart dresses of bright colours shaded in clouds, embroidered with monsters of gold or silver, are reserved by the great ladies for home use on state occasions ; or else they are used on the stage for the dancers and the courtesans.

Like all Japanese women, Chrysanthème carries a quantity of things in her long sleeves, in which pockets are cunningly hidden. There she keeps letters, various notes written on delicate sheets of rice-paper, prayer amulets drawn up by the bonzes ; and above all a number of squares of a silky paper which she puts to the most unexpected uses,—to dry a tea-cup, to hold the damp stalk of a flower, or to blow her quaint little nose, when the necessity presents itself. After the operation she at once crumples up the piece of paper, rolls it into a ball, and throws it out of the window with disgust.

The very smartest people in Japan blow their noses in this manner.

XL.

CHANCE has favoured us with a friendship as singular as it is rare: that of the head bonzes of the temple of the *Jumping Tortoise,* where we had witnessed last month such a surprising pilgrimage.

The approach to this place is as solitary now as it was thronged and bustling on the evenings of the festival; and in broad daylight one is surprised at the deathlike decay of the religious surroundings which at night had seemed so full of life. Not a creature to be seen on the time-worn granite steps; not a creature beneath the vast sumptuous porticoes; the colours, the gold-work are dim with dust. To reach the temple one must cross several deserted courtyards terraced on the mountain side, pass through several solemn gateways, and up and up endless stairs, rising far above the town and the noises of humanity into a sacred region filled with innumerable tombs. On all the pavements, in all the walls, lichen and stonecrop; and over all the grey tint of extreme age spreads everywhere like a fall of ashes.

In a side temple near the entrance is enthroned a colossal Buddha seated in his lotus—a gilded idol some forty-five or sixty feet high, mounted on an enormous pedestal of bronze.

At length appears the last doorway with the two traditional giants, guardians of the sacred court, which stand the one on the right hand, the other on the left, shut up like wild beasts each one in a cage of iron. They are in attitudes of fury, with fists upraised as if to strike, and features atrociously fierce and distorted. Their bodies are covered all over with bullets of crumbled paper which have been aimed at them through the bars, and which have stuck to their monstrous limbs like a white leprosy: this is the manner in which the faithful strive to appease them, by conveying to them their prayers written upon delicate leaflets by the pious bonzes.

Passing between these alarming scarecrows one reaches the innermost court. The residence of our friends is on the right, the great hall of the pagoda is before us.

In this paved court are bronze torch-holders as high as turrets. Here too stand, and have stood for centuries, cyca palms with fresh green plumes, their numerous stalks curving with a heavy symmetry, like the branches of massive candelabra. The temple, which is open along its entire length, is dark and mysterious, with touches of gilding in distant corners melting away into the gloom. In the very remotest part are seated idols, and from outside one can vaguely see their clasped hands and air of rapt mysticism; in front are the altars, loaded with marvellous vases in metal-work, whence spring graceful clusters of gold and silver lotus. From the very entrance one is greeted by the sweet odour of the incense-sticks unceasingly burnt by the priests before the gods.

To penetrate into the dwelling of our friends the bonzes, which is situated on the right hand side as you enter, is by no means an easy matter.

A monster of the fish tribe, but having claws

and horns, is hung over their door by iron
chains ; at the least breath of wind he swings
creakingly. We pass beneath him and enter
the first immense and lofty hall, dimly lighted,
in the corners of which gleam gilded idols, bells,
and incomprehensible objects of religious use.

Quaint little creatures, choir boys or pupils,
come forward with a doubtful welcome to ask
what is wanted.

"*Matsou-San ! ! Donata-San ! !*" they repeat, much astonished, when they understand
to whom we wish to be conducted. Oh! no,
impossible, they cannot be seen ; they are

resting or are in contemplation. "*Orimas!
Orimas!*" say they, clasping their hands and
sketching a genuflection or two to make us

understand better. (They are at prayer! the
most profound prayer!)

We insist, speak more imperatively; even
slip off our shoes like people determined to
take no refusal.

At last Matsou-San and Donata-San make
their appearance from the tranquil depths of
their bonze-house. They are dressed in black
crape and their heads are shaved. Smiling,
amiable, full of excuses, they offer us their
hands, and we follow with our feet bare like
theirs to the interior of their mysterious
dwelling, through a series of empty rooms
spread with mats of the most unimpeachable
whiteness. The successive halls are separated
one from the other only by bamboo curtains
of exquisite delicacy, caught back by tassels
and cords of red silk.

The whole wainscoting of the interior is of
the same wood, of a pale yellow colour
joinered with extreme nicety, without the least
ornament, the least carving ; everything seems
new and unused, as though it had never been
touched by human hand. At distant intervals
in this studied bareness, costly little stools,
marvellously inlaid, uphold some antique bronze
monster or a vase of flowers; on the walls
hang a few masterly sketches, vaguely tinted
in Indian ink, drawn upon strips of grey paper
most accurately cut but without the slightest
attempt at a frame ; this is all : not a seat, not
a cushion, not a scrap of furniture. It is the
very acme of studied simplicity, of elegance

made out of nothing, of the most immaculate
and incredible cleanliness.   And while following
the bonzes through this long suite of empty
halls, we are struck by their contrast with the
overflow of knick-knacks scattered about our
rooms in France, and we take a sudden dislike
to the profusion and crowding delighted in at
home.

The spot where this silent march of barefooted folk comes to an end, the spot where we
are to seat ourselves in the delightful coolness of
a semi-darkness, is an interior verandah opening upon an artificial site ; we might suppose it
were the bottom of a well ; it is a miniature
garden no bigger than the opening of an
oubliette, overhung on all sides by the crushing
height of the mountain and receiving from
on high but the dim light of dream-land.
Nevertheless here is simulated a great natural
ravine in all its wild grandeur : here are
caverns, abrupt rocks, a torrent, a cascade,
islands. The trees, dwarfed by a Japanese
process of which we have not the secret, have
tiny little leaves on their decrepit and knotty
branches. A pervading hue of the mossy
green of antiquity harmonises all this medley,
which is undoubtedly centuries old.

Families of gold-fish swim round and round

in the clear water, and tiny tortoises (*jumpers* probably) sleep upon the granite islands which are of the same colour as their own grey shell.

There are even blue dragon-flies which have ventured to descend, heaven knows from whence, and alight with quivering wings upon the miniature water-lilies.

Our friends the bonzes, notwithstanding an unctuousness of manner thoroughly ecclesiastical, are very ready to laugh,—a simple, pleased, childish laughter ; plump, chubby, shaven and shorn, they dearly love our French liqueurs and know how to take a joke.

We talk first of one thing and then another. To the tranquil music of their little cascade, I launch out before them with phrases of the most erudite Japanese, I try the effect of a few tenses of verbs : *desideratives, concessives, hypo-thetics in ba*. Whilst they chat they dispatch the affairs of the church, the order of services sealed with complicated seals for inferior pagodas situated in the neighbourhood ; or trace little prayers with a cunning paint-brush as medical remedies to be swallowed as pills by invalids at a distance. With their white and dimpled hands they play with a fan as cleverly as any woman, and when we have tasted different native drinks flavoured with essences of flowers, they bring up as a finish a bottle of *Bénédictine* or *Chartreuse*, for they appreciate the liqueurs composed by their Western colleagues.

When they come on board to return our visits, they by no means disdain to fasten their great round spectacles on their flat noses in order to inspect the profane drawings in our illustrated papers, the *Vie Parisienne* for instance. And it is even with a certain complacency that they let their fingers linger upon the pictures which represent the ladies.

The religious ceremonies in their great temple are magnificent, and to one of these we are now invited. At the sound of the gong they make their entrance before the idols with a stately ritual ; twenty or thirty priests officiate in gala costumes, with genuflections, clapping of hands and movements to and fro, which look like the figures of some mystic quadrille.

But for all that, let the sanctuary be ever so immense and imposing in its sombre gloom, the idols ever so superb, all seems in Japan but a mere semblance of grandeur. A hopeless **pettiness**, an irresistible feeling of the **ludicrous**, lies at the bottom of all things.

And then the congregation is not conducive to thoughtful contemplation, for among it we generally discover some acquaintance: my mother-in-law, or a cousin, or the woman from the china-shop who sold us a vase only yesterday. Charming little mousmés, monkeyish-looking old ladies enter with their smoking-boxes, their gaily-daubed parasols, their curtsies, their little cries and exclamations; prattling, complimenting each other, full of restless movement, and having the greatest difficulty in maintaining a serious demeanour.

XLI.

CHRYSANTHÈME, for the first time, paid me
a visit on board ship to-day, chaperoned by
Madame Prune, and followed by my youngest
sister-in-law, Mdlle. La Neige. These ladies
had the tranquil manners of the highest gentility.

In my cabin is a great Buddha on his throne,
and before him a lacquer tray, on which my
faithful sailor servant places any small change
he may find lying loose in the pockets of my
clothes. Madame Prune, whose mind is much
swayed by mysticism, at once supposed herself
before a regular altar; in the gravest manner

possible she addressed a brief prayer to the
god ; then, drawing out her purse (which,
according to custom, was attached to her sash
behind her back, along with her little pipe and
tobacco-pouch), placed a pious offering in the
tray, while executing a low curtsey.

They remained on their best behaviour all
through the visit.   But when the moment of
departure came, Chrysanthème, who would
not go away without seeing Yves, asked for
him with a thinly-veiled persistency which was
remarkable.   Yves, for whom I then sent, made
himself particularly charming to her, so much
so, that this time I felt a shade of more serious
annoyance ; I even asked myself whether the
laughably pitiable ending, which I had hitherto
vaguely foreseen, might not, after all, soon break
upon us.

Ross,

XLII.

I MET yesterday, in an old and ruined quarter
of the town, a perfectly exquisite mousmé,
charmingly dressed ; a fresh note of colour
against the dark background of decayed
buildings.

It was quite at the farthest end of Nagasaki,
in the most ancient part of the town.   In this
region are trees centuries old, ancient temples
of Buddha, of Amiddah, of Benten, or Kwanon,
with steep and pompous roofs ; monsters carved
in granite sit there in courtyards silent as the
grave, where the grass grows between the
paving-stones. This deserted quarter is tra-
versed by a narrow torrent running in a deep

channel, across which are thrown little curved bridges with granite balustrades eaten away by lichen. All the objects there wear the strange grimace, the quaint arrangement familiar to us in the most antique Japanese drawings.

I walked through it all at the burning hour of midday, and saw not a soul, unless indeed, through the open windows of the bonze-houses, I caught sight of some few priests, guardians of tombs or sanctuaries, taking their siesta under their dark-blue gauze nets.

All at once this little mousmé appeared, a little above me, just at the point of the arch of one of these bridges carpeted with grey moss ; she was in full light, in full sunshine, and stood out in brilliant clearness, like a fairy vision, against the background of old black temples and deep shadows. She was holding her dress together with one hand, gathering it close round her ankles to give herself an air of greater slimness. Over her quaint little head, her round umbrella with its thousand ribs threw a great halo of blue and red, edged with black, and an oleander full of flowers growing among the stones of the bridge spread its glory beside her, bathed, like herself, in the sunshine. Behind this youthful figure and this flowering shrub all was black-ness. Upon the pretty red and blue parasol great white letters formed this inscription, much

used among the mousmés, and which I have
learned to recognise : *Stop! clouds, to see her
pass by*. And it was really worth the trouble
to stop and look at this exquisite little person,
of a type so ideally Japanese.

However, it will not do to stop too long
and be ensnared,—it would only be another
take-in. A doll like the rest, evidently,
an ornament for a china shelf, and nothing
more. While I gaze at her, I say to myself
that Chrysanthème, appearing in this same
place, with this dress, this play of light, and this
aureole of sunshine, would produce just as
delightful an effect.

For Chrysanthème is pretty, there can be
no doubt about it. Yesterday evening, in fact,
I positively admired her. It was quite night;
we were returning with the usual escort of little
married couples like our own, from the inevitable tour of the tea-houses and bazaars.
While the other mousmés walked along hand
in hand, adorned with new silver top-knots
which they had succeeded in having presented
to them, and amusing themselves with playthings, she, pleading fatigue, followed, half
reclining, in a djin carriage. We had placed
beside her great bunches of flowers destined
to fill our vases, late iris and long-stemmed
lotus, the last of the season, already smelling of

autumn. And it was really very pretty to see this Japanese girl in her little car, lying carelessly among all these water-flowers, lighted by gleams of ever-changing colours, as they chanced from the lanterns we met or passed. If, on the evening of my arrival in Japan, any one had pointed her out to me, and said: "That shall be your mousmé," there cannot be a doubt I should have been charmed. In reality, however, no, I am not charmed; it is only Chrysanthème, always Chrysanthème, nothing but Chrysanthème: a mere plaything to laugh at, a little creature of finical forms and thoughts, that the agency of M. Kangourou has supplied me with.

XLIII.

In our house, the water used for drinking, making tea, and lesser washing purposes, is kept in large white china tubs, decorated with paintings representing blue fish borne along by a swift current through distorted rushes.   In order to keep them cool, the tubs are placed out of doors on Madame Prune's roof, at a place where we can, from the top of our projecting balcony, easily reach them by stretching out the arm. A real godsend for all the thirsty cats in the neighbourhood on the fine summer nights is this corner of the roof with our bedaubed tubs, and it proves a delightful trysting-place for them, after all their caterwauling and long solitary rambles on the top of the walls.

I had thought it my duty to warn Yves the first time he wished to drink this water.

" Oh ! " he replied, rather surprised, "cats do you say ? they are not dirty ! "

On this point Chrysanthème and I agree with him : we do not consider cats as unclean animals, and we do not object to drink after them.

Yves considers Chrysanthème much in the same light. " She is not dirty, either," he says ; and he willingly drinks after her, out of the same cup, putting her in the same category with the cats.

Well, these china tubs are one of the daily preoccupations of our household : in the evening, when we return from our walk, after the clamber up which makes us thirsty, and Madame L'Heure's waffles, which we have been eating to beguile the way, we always find them empty. It seems impossible for Madame Prune, or Mdlle. Oyouki, or their young servant Mdlle. Dédé,* to

* *Dédé-San* means " Miss Young Girl," a very common name.

have forethought enough to fill them while it is still daylight. And when we are late in returning home, these three ladies are asleep, so we are obliged to attend to the business ourselves.

We must therefore open all the closed doors, put on our boots, and go down into the garden to draw water.

As Chrysanthème would die of frig all alone in the dark, in the midst of the trees and buzzing of the insects, I am obliged to accompany her to the well. For this expedition we require a light, and must seek among the quantity of lanterns purchased at Madame Très-Propre's booth, which have been thrown night after night into the bottom of one of our little paper closets ; but alas, all the candles are burnt down ! I thought as much ! Well, we must resolutely take the first lantern to hand, and stick a fresh candle on the iron point at the bottom ; Chrysanthème puts forth all her strength, the candle splits, breaks ; the mousmé pricks her fingers, pouts and whimpers. Such is the inevitable scene that takes place every evening, and delays our retiring to rest under the dark blue gauze net for a good quarter of an hour ; while the cicalas on the roof seem to mock us with their ceaseless song.

All this, which I should find amusing in anyone else,—anyone I loved—provokes me in her.

XLIV.

A WEEK has passed by peacefully enough, during which I have written down nothing.

Little by little I am becoming accustomed to my Japanese household, to the strangeness of the language, costumes, and faces. For the last three weeks, no letters have arrived from Europe; they have no doubt miscarried, and their absence contributes, as is usually the case, to throw a veil of oblivion over the past.

Every day, therefore, I faithfully climb up to

my villa, sometimes by beautiful star-lit nights, sometimes through stormy downpours of rain. Every morning as the sound of Madame Prune's chanted prayer rises through the reverberating air, I awake and go down towards the sea, by the grassy pathways full of dew.

The chief occupation in this Japanese country, seems to be a perpetual hunt after curios. We sit down on the mattings, in the antique-sellers' little booths, take a cup of tea with the salesmen, and rummage with our own hands in the cupboards and chests, where many a fantastic piece of old rubbish is huddled away. The bargaining, much discussed, is laughingly carried on for several days, as though we were trying to play off some excellent little practical joke upon each other.

I really make a sad abuse of the adjective *little*, I am quite aware of it, but how can I do otherwise? In describing this country, the temptation is great to use it ten times in every written line. Little, finical, affected,—all Japan is contained, both physically and morally, in these three words.

My purchases are accumulating up there, in my little wood and paper house; but how much

more Japanese it really was, in its bare empti-
ness, such as M. Sucre and Madame Prune had
conceived it.   There are now many lamps of a
religious shape hanging from the ceiling ; many
stools and many vases, as many gods and god-
desses as in a pagoda.

There is even a little Shintoist altar, before
which Madame Prune has not been able to
restrain her feelings, and before which she
has fallen down and chanted her prayers in her
bleating old nanny-goat voice :

"Wash me clean from all my impurity, oh
Ama-Térace-Omi-Kami, as one washes away
uncleanness in the river of Kamo."

Alas for poor Ama-Térace-Omi-Kami to have
to wash away the impurities of Madame
Prune ! What a tedious and ungrateful task ! !

Chrysanthème, who is a Buddhist, prays
sometimes in the evening before lying down ;
although overcome with sleep, she prays clapping her hands before the largest of our gilded
idols. But she smiles with a childish disre-
spect for her Buddha, directly her prayer is
ended. I know that she has also a certain
veneration for her *Ottokés* (the Spirits of her
ancestors), whose rather sumptuous altar is set
up at her mother's, Madame Renoncule's. She
asks for their blessings, for fortune and wisdom.

Who can make out her ideas about the gods, or about death? Does she possess a soul? Does she think she has one? Her religion is an obscure chaos of theogonies as old as the world, treasured up out of respect for ancient customs; and of more recent ideas

about the blessed final annihilation, imported from India at the epoch of our middle ages by saintly Chinese missionnaries. The bonzes themselves are puzzled; what a muddle, therefore, must not all this become, when jumbled together in the childish brain of a sleepy mousmé?

Two very insignificant episodes have somewhat attached me to her—(bonds of this kind seldom fail to draw closer in the end). The first occasion was as follows :—

Madame Prune one day brought forth a relic of her gay youth, a tortoiseshell comb of rare transparency, one of those combs that it is good style to place on the summit of the head, lightly poised, scarcely stuck at all in the hair, with all the teeth showing. Taking it out of a pretty little lacquered box, she held it up in the air

and blinked her eyes, looking through it at the sky—a bright summer sky—as one does to examine the quality of a precious stone.

"Here is," she said, "an object of great value that you should offer to your little wife."

My mousmé, very much taken by it, admired the clearness of the comb and its graceful shape.

The lacquered box, however, pleased me most. On the cover was a wonderful painting in gold on gold, representing a field of rice, seen very close, on a windy day: a tangle of ears and grass beaten down and twisted by a terrible squall; here and there, between the distorted stalks, the muddy earth of the rice-swamp was visible; there were even little pools of water, produced by bits of the transparent lacquer on which tiny particles of gold seemed to float about like chaff in a thick liquid; two or three insects, which required a microscope to be well seen, were clinging in a terrified manner to the rushes, and the whole picture was no larger than a woman's hand.

As for Madame Prune's comb, I confess it left me indifferent, and I turned a deaf ear, thinking it very insignificant and expensive. Then Chrysanthème answered mournfully:

"No, thank you, I don't want it; take it away, dear Madame Prune."

And at the same time she heaved a deep sigh, full of meaning, which plainly said:

" He is not so fond of me as all that.—Useless to bother him."

I immediately made the wished-for purchase.

Later on, when Chrysanthème will have become an old monkey like Madame Prune, with her black teeth and long orisons, she, in her turn, will retail that comb to some fine lady of a fresh generation.

On another occasion the sun had given me a headache ; I lay on the floor resting my head on my snake-skin pillow. My eyes were dim, and everything appeared to turn round : the open verandah, the big expanse of luminous evening sky, and a variety of kites hovering against its background ; I felt myself vibrating painfully to the rhythmical sound of the cicalas which filled the atmosphere.

She, crouching down by my side, strove to relieve me by a Japanese process, pressing with all her might on my temples with her little thumbs and turning them rapidly round, as though she were boring a hole with a gimlet. She had become quite hot and red over this hard work, which procured me real comfort, something similar to the dreamy intoxication of opium.

Then, anxious and fearful lest J should have

an attack of fever, she rolled into a pellet and
thrust into my mouth a very efficacious prayer
written on rice-paper, which she carefully kept
in the lining of one of her sleeves.

Well, I swallowed that prayer without a smile,
anxious not to hurt her feelings or shake her
funny little faith.

XLV.

To-day, Yves, my mousmé and myself went to the best photographer in Nagasaki, to be taken in a group together.

We shall send the photograph to France. Yves already smiles as he thinks of his wife's astonishment when she sees Chrysanthème's little face between us two, and he wonders what explanation he will give her.

"Well, I will just say it is one of your friends, that's all!"

There are, in Japan, photographers in the

style of our own, with this one difference, that
they are Japanese, and inhabit Japanese houses.
The one we design to honour to-day carries on
his profession in the suburbs, in that ancient
quarter of big trees and gloomy pagodas where,
the other day, I met the pretty little mousmé.
His signboard, written in several languages, is
stuck up against a wall on the edge of the little
torrent which, rushing down from the green
mountain above, is crossed by many a curved
bridge of old granite and lined on either side
by light bamboos or oleanders in full bloom.

It is astonishing and puzzling to find a photographer perched there, in the very heart of old
Japan.

We have come at the wrong moment; there
is a file of people at the door. Long rows of
djins' cars are stationed there, awaiting the
customers they have brought, who will all have
their turn before us. The runners, naked and
tatooed, carefully combed in sleek bands and
shiny chignons, are chatting together, smoking
little pipes, or bathing their muscular legs in
the fresh water of the torrent.

The courtyard is irreproachably Japanese,
with its lanterns and dwarf trees. But the
studio where one sits might be in Paris or

Pontoise; the self-same chair in "old oak," the same faded "poufs," plaster columns and pasteboard rocks.

The people who are being *taken* at this moment are two ladies of quality, evidently mother and daughter, who are sitting together for a cabinet-sized portrait, with accessories of Louis XV. time. A strange group this, the first great ladies of this country I have seen so near, with their long aristocratic faces, dull, lifeless, almost grey by dint of rice-powder, and their mouths painted heart-shape in vivid carmine. Withal an undeniable look of good breeding that strongly impresses us, notwithstanding the intrinsic differences of races and acquired notions.

They scanned Chrysanthème with an obvious look of scorn, although her costume was as ladylike as their own. For my part, I could not take my eyes off these two creatures; they captivated me like incomprehensible things that one had never seen before. Their fragile bodies, outlandishly graceful in posture, are lost in stiff materials and redundant sashes, of which the ends droop like tired wings. They make me think, I know not why, of great rare insects; the extraordinary patterns on their garments have something of the dark motley of

night-moths.   Above all, the mystery of their
tiny slits of eyes, drawn back and up so far
that the tight-drawn lids can scarcely open ;
the mystery of their expression, which seems
to denote inner thoughts of a silly, vague,
complacent absurdity, a world of ideas absolutely closed to ourselves.   And I think as I
gaze at them : " How far we are from this
Japanese people ! how utterly dissimilar are
our races ! "

Then we have to let several English sailors
pass before us, decked out in their white drill
clothes, fresh, fat and pink like little sugar
figures, who attitudinise in a sheepish manner
round the shafts of the columns.

At last it is our turn ; Chrysanthème slowly
settles herself in a very affected style, turning
in the points of her toes as much as possible,
according to the fashion.

And on the negative we are shown we look
like a supremely ridiculous little family drawn
up in a line by a common photographer at a fair.

XLVI.

THIS evening Yves is off duty three hours earlier than myself; from time to time this is the case, according to the arrangement of the watches. On those occasions he lands the first, and goes up to wait for me at Diou-djen-dji.

From the deck I can see him through the glasses, climbing up the green mountain path;

he walks with a brisk, rapid step, almost running ; what a hurry he seems in to rejoin little Chrysanthème.

When I arrive, at about nine o'clock, I find him seated on the floor, in the middle of my rooms, with naked torso (this is here a sufficiently proper costume for private life, I admit). Around him are grouped Chrysanthème, Oyouki, and Mdlle. Dédé the maid, all eagerly rubbing his back with little blue towels decorated with storks and humorous subjects.

Good heavens, what can he have been doing to be so hot, and have put himself in such a state ?

He tells me that near our house, a little higher up the mountain, he has discovered a fencing gallery : that till nightfall he had been engaged in a fencing bout against Japanese, who fought with two-handed swords, springing like cats, as is the custom of their country. With his French method of fencing he had given them a thorough good drubbing.   Upon which, with many a low bow, they had shown him their admiration by bringing him a quantity of nice little iced things to drink.   All this combined had thrown him into a fearful perspiration.

Ah, very well. Nevertheless this did not quite explain to me.

He is delighted with his evening; intends to go and amuse himself every day by beating them; he even thinks of taking pupils.

Once his back dried, they all together, the three mousmés and himself, play at Japanese "*pigeon vole.*" Really I could not wish for anything more innocent, or more correct in every respect.

Charles N——— and Madame Jonquille his wife, arrived unexpectedly at about ten o'clock. (They were wandering about in the dark shrubberies in our neighbourhood, and, seeing our lights, came up to us.)

They intend to finish the evening at the tea-house " of the Toads," and they try to induce us to go and drink some iced sherbets with them. It is at least an hour's walk from here, on the other side of the town, half way up the hill, in the gardens of the large pagoda dedicated to Osueva; but they stick to their idea, pretending that in this clear night and bright moonlight, we shall have a lovely view from the terrace of the temple.

Lovely, I have no doubt, but we had intended going to bed. However, be it so, let us go with them.

We hire five djins and five cars down below, in the principal street, in front of Madame Très-Propre's shop, who, for this late expedition, chooses for us her largest round lanterns, — big, red balloons, decorated with star-fish, seaweed, and green sharks.

It is nearly eleven o'clock when we make our start. In the central quarters the virtuous Niponese are already closing their little booths, putting out their lamps, shutting the wooden framework, drawing their paper panels.

Further on, in the old-fashioned suburban streets, all is shut up long ago, and our carts roll on through the black night. We cry out

to our djins: "Ayakou! ayakou!" ("Quick!
quick!") and they run as hard as they can, uttering little shrieks, like some merry animal full of

wild gaiety. We rush like a whirlwind through
the darkness, all five in Indian file, dashing
and jolting over the old uneven flagstones,
dimly lighted up by our red balloons fluttering

at the end of their bamboo stems. From time
to time some Niponese, night-capped in his
blue kerchief, opens a window to see who these
noisy madcaps can be, dashing by so rapidly
and so late. Or else some faint glimmer,
thrown by us on our passage, discovers the
hideous smile of a large stone animal seated at
the gate of a pagoda.

At last we arrive at the foot of Osueva's
temple, and, leaving our djins with our little
gigs, we clamber up the gigantic steps, completely deserted at this hour of the night.

Chrysanthème, who always likes to play
the part of a tired little girl, of a spoilt and
pouting child, ascends slowly between Yves
and myself, clinging to our arms.

Jonquille, on the contrary, skips up like a
bird, amusing herself by counting the endless
steps :

"Hitôts'! F'tâts'! Mits'! Yôts'! ("One!
two! three! four!") she exclaims, springing up
by a series of little light bounds.

"Itsôûts'! Moûts'! Nanâts! Yâts'! Koko-
nôts'!" ("Five! six! seven! eight! nine!")

She lays a great stress on the accentuations,

as though to make the numbers sound even more droll.

A little silver aigrette glitters in her beautiful black chignon; her delicate and graceful figure seems strangely fantastic, and the darkness that envelops us conceals the fact that her face is almost ugly, and almost without eyes.

This evening Chrysanthème and Jonquille really look like little fairies; at certain moments the most insignificant Japanese have this appearance, by dint of whimsical elegance and ingenious arrangement.

The granite stairs, immense, deserted, uniformly grey under the nocturnal sky, seem to vanish into the empty space above us, and when we turn round, to disappear in the depths beneath, to fall with the dizzy rapidity of a dream into the abyss below. On the sloping steps the black shadows of the gateways through which we must pass stretch out inordinately; and the shadows, which seem to be broken at each projecting step, bear on all their extent the regular creases of a fan. The porticos stand up separately, rising one above the other; their wonderful shapes are at once remarkably simple and studiously affected; their outlines stand out sharp and distinct, having nevertheless the vague appearance of all very large objects in the pale moonlight. The curved architraves rise up at each extremity like two menacing horns, pointing upwards towards the far-off blue canopy of sky bespangled with stars, as though they would communicate to the gods the knowledge they have acquired in the depths of their foundations from the earth, full of sepulchres and death, which surrounds them.

We are, indeed, a very small group, lost now in the immensity of the colossal acclivity as we move onwards, lighted partly by the wan moon on high, partly by the red lanterns we hold in our hands, ever floating at the end of their long sticks.

A deep silence reigns in the precincts of the temple, the sound of the insects even is hushed as we ascend higher. A sort of reverence, a kind of religious fear steals over us, and, at the same moment, a delicious coolness suddenly pervades the air, and passes over us.

On entering the courtyard above, we feel a little daunted. Here we find the horse in jade, and the china turrets. The enclosing walls make it the more gloomy, and our arrival seems to disturb I know not what mysterious council held between the spirits of the air and the visible symbols that are there, chimeras and monsters lit up by the blue rays of the moon.

We turn to the left, and go through the terraced gardens, to reach the tea-house " of the Toads," which this evening is our goal ; we find it shut up—I expected as much—closed and dark, at this hour ! We drum all together on the door ; in the most coaxing tones we call by name the waiting-maids we know so well : Mdlle. Transparente, Mdlle. Etoile, Mdlle. Rosée-matinale, and Mdlle. Marguerite-reine. Not an answer. Goodbye perfumed sherbets and frosted beans !

In front of the little archery-house, our mousmés suddenly start on one side, terrified, and declaring that there is a dead body on the ground. Yes, indeed, someone is lying there. We cautiously examine the place by the light of our red balloons, carefully held out at arm's length for fear of this dead man ; it is only the marksman, he who on the 14th of July chose such magnificent arrows for Chrysanthème ; and he sleeps, good man, with his chignon somewhat dishevelled, a sound sleep, which it would be cruel to disturb.

Let us go to the end of the terrace, contemplate the roadstead at our feet, and then return home. To-night the harbour looks only like a dark and sinister rent, which the moonbeams cannot fathom,—a yawning crevasse opening into the very bowels of the earth, at the bottom of which lie faint and small glimmers, an assembly of glow-worms in a ditch—the lights of the different vessels lying at anchor.

XLVII.

It is the middle of the night, somewhere
about two in the morning. Our night-lamps
are burning still, a little dimly, in front of our
peaceful idols. Chrysanthème wakes me suddenly, and I turn to look at her: she has
raised herself on one arm, and her face expresses
the most intense terror; she makes me a sign,
without daring to speak, that someone is near,
or something, creeping up to us. What ill-
timed visit is this? A feeling of fear gains
possession of me also. I have a rapid impression of some immense unknown danger, in this
isolated spot, in this strange country of which I
do not even yet comprehend the inhabitants

and the mysteries.   It must be something very frightful, to hold her there, rooted to the spot, half dead with fright, she who *does* comprehend all these things.

It would seem to be outside ; it is coming from the garden ; with trembling hand she indicates to me that it will come through the verandah, over Madame Prune's roof.   Certainly, I can hear faint noises, and they do approach nearer.

I suggest to her :

" *Neko-San ?* " (" It is Messrs. the cats ? ")

"No!" she replies, still terrified and in an alarming tone.

" *Bakémono-Sama ?* " (" Is it my lords the ghosts ? ") I have already the Japanese habit of expressing myself with excessive politeness.

" No !! *Dorobo ! !* " (" Thieves ! ! ")

Thieves !   Ah ! this is better ; I much prefer this to a visit such as I have just been dreading in the sudden awakening from sleep : from ghosts or spirits of the dead ; thieves, that is to say, worthy fellows very much alive, and having undoubtedly, in as much as they are Japanese thieves, faces of the most meritorious oddity. I am not in the least frightened, now that I know precisely what to expect, and we will immediately set to work to ascertain the truth, for something is decidedly moving on Madame Prune's roof ; some one is walking upon it.

I open one of our wooden panels and look out.

I can see only a vast expanse, calm, peaceful, and exquisite under the full brilliancy of the moonlight; sleeping Japan lulled by the sonorous song of the grasshoppers is charming indeed to-night, and the free pure air is delicious to breathe.

Chrysanthème, half hidden behind my shoulder, listens tremblingly, peering forward to examine the gardens and the roofs with dilated eyes like a frightened cat. No, nothing! not a thing moves. Here and there are a few strangely substantial shadows, which at the first glance were not easy to explain, but which turn out to be real shadows, thrown by bits of wall, by boughs of trees, and which preserve an extremely reassuring stillness. Everything seems absolutely tranquil, and profound silence reigns in the dreamy vagueness which moonlight sheds over all.

Nothing; nothing to be seen anywhere. It was Messrs. the cats after all, or perhaps my ladies the owls; sounds increase in volume in the most amazing manner at night, in this house of ours.

Let us close the panel again carefully, as a measure of prudence, and then light a lantern and go downstairs to see if there may be any one hidden in corners, and if the doors are tightly shut: in short, to reassure Chrysanthème we will go the round of the house.

Behold us then, on tip-toe, searching together every hole and corner of the house, which, to judge by its foundations, must be very ancient, notwithstanding the fragile appearance of its

panels of white paper. It contains the blackest of cavities, little vaulted cellars with worm-eaten beams; cupboards for rice which smell of mould and decay; mysterious hollows where lies accumulated the dust of centuries. In the middle of the night, and during a hunt for thieves, this part of the house, as yet unknown to me, has an ugly look.

Noiselessly we step across the apartment of our landlord and landlady. Chrysanthème drags me by the hand, and I allow myself to be led. There they are, sleeping in a row under their blue gauze tent, lighted by the night-lamps burning before the altars of their ancestors. Ha! I observe that they are arranged in an order which might give rise to gossip.

First comes Mdlle. Oyouki, very taking in her attitude of rest.   Then Madame Prune, who sleeps with her mouth wide open, showing her rows of blackened teeth; from her throat arises an intermittent sound like the grunting of a sow.

Oh! poor Madame Prune! how hideous she is!! Next, M. Sucre, a mere mummy for the time being.   And finally, at his side, last of the row, is their servant, Mdlle. Dédé!!!

The gauze hanging over them throws reflections as of the sea upon them; one might suppose them victims drowned in an aquarium. And withal the sacred lamps, the altar crowded with strange Shintoist symbols, give a mock religious air to this family picture.

Honi soit qui mal y pense, but why is not that servant-girl rather laid by the side of her mistresses? Now, when we on the floor above offer our hospitality to Yves, we are careful to place ourselves under our mosquito-net in a more correct style.

One corner, which as a last resort we inspect, inspires me with a certain amount of apprehension. It is a low, mysterious loft, against the door of which is stuck, as a thing no longer wanted, a very old pious image: *Kwanon with the thousand arms*, and *Kwanon with the horses' head*, seated among clouds and flames, and horrible both of them to behold, with their spectral grin.

We open the door, and Chrysanthème starts back uttering a fearful cry. I should have thought the robbers were there, had I not seen a little grey creature, rapid and noiseless, rush by her and disappear; a young rat that had been eating rice on the top of a shelf, and, in its alarm, had dashed in her face.

XLVIII.

YVES has dropped his silver whistle in the sea, the whistle so absolutely indispensable for the manœuvres; and we search the town through all day long, followed by Chrysanthème and Mdlles. La Neige and La Lune, her sisters, in the endeavour to procure another.

It is, however, very difficult to find such a thing in Nagasaki; above all, very difficult to explain in Japanese what is a sailor's whistle of the traditional shape, curved and with a little ball at the end to modulate the trills and the various sounds of official orders. For three

hours we are sent from shop to shop ; at each
one they pretend to understand perfectly what
is wanted and trace on tissue-paper, with a paint-
brush, the addresses of the shops where we
shall without fail meet with what we require,—
away we go, full of hope, only to encounter
some fresh mystification, till our breathless djins
get quite bewildered.

They understand admirably that we want a
thing that will make a noise, music in short ;
thereupon they offer us instruments of every and
the most unexpected shape,—squeakers for
Punch-and-Judy voices, dog-whistles, trumpets.
Each time it is something more and more
absurd, so that at last we are overcome with
uncontrollable fits of laughter. Last of all, an
aged Japanese optician, who assumes a most
knowing air, a look of sublime wisdom, goes off
to forage in his back shop, and brings to light
a steam fog-horn, a relict from some wrecked
steamer.

After dinner, the chief event of the evening
is a deluge of rain which takes us by surprise as
we leave the tea-houses, on our return from our
fashionable stroll. It so happened that we
were a large party, having with us several
mousmé guests, and from the moment that the

rain began to fall from the skies, as if out of
a watering-pot turned upside down, the band
became disorganized. The mousmés run off,
with birdlike cries, and take refuge under
door-ways, in the shops, under the hoods of the
djins.

Then, before long,—-when the shops shut up
in haste, when the emptied streets are flooded,
and almost black, and the paper lanterns, piteous
objects, wet through and extinguished,—I find
myself, I know not how it happens, flattened
against a wall, under the projecting eaves, alone
in the company of Mdlle. Fraise, my cousin,
who is crying bitterly because her fine dress is
wet through. And in the noise of the rain,
which is still falling and splashing everything ;
with the spouts and gutters, which in the
darkness plaintively murmur like running
streams, the town appears to me suddenly an
abode of the gloomiest sadness.

The shower is soon over, and the mousmés
come out of their holes like so many mice ; they
look for each other, call each other, and their
little voices take the singular melancholy,
dragging inflections they assume whenever
they have to call from afar.

" Hi ! Mdlle. Lu-u-u-u-une ! ! "

"Hi! Madame Jonqui-i-i-i-ille!!"

They shout from one to the other their outlandish names, prolonging them indefinitely in
the now silent night, in the reverberations of
the damp air after the great summer rain.

At length they are all collected and united
again, these tiny personages with narrow eyes
and no brains, and we return to Diou-djen-dji
all wet through.

For the third time, we have Yves sleeping
beside us under our blue tent.

There is a great row soon after midnight in
the apartment beneath us : our landlord's family
returning from a pilgrimage to a far-distant
temple of the Goddess of Grace. (Although
Madame Prune is a Shintoist, she reveres
this deity, who, scandal says, watched over her
youth.) A moment after, Mdlle. Oyouki bursts
into our room like a rocket, bringing, on a charming little tray, sweetmeats which have been
blessed and bought at the gates of the temple
yonder, on purpose for us, and which we must
positively eat at once, before the virtue is gone
out of them. Scarcely rousing ourselves, we
absorb these little edibles flavoured with sugar
and pepper, and return a great many sleepy
thanks.

Yves sleeps quietly on this occasion, without dealing any blows to the floor or the panels either with fists or feet. He has hung his watch on one of the hands of our gilded idol in order to be more sure of seeing the hour at any time of the night, by the light of the sacred lamps. He gets up betimes in the morning, asking : " Well, did I behave properly ? " and dresses in haste, preoccupied about duty and the roll-call.

Outside, no doubt, it is daylight already : through the tiny holes which time has pierced in our wooden panels, threads of morning light penetrate our chamber, and in the atmosphere of our room where night still lingers, they trace vague white rays. Soon, when the sun shall have risen, these rays will lengthen and become beautifully golden. The cocks and the cicalas make themselves heard, and now Madame Prune will begin her mystic drone.

Nevertheless, out of politeness for Yves-San, Chrysanthème lights a lantern and escorts him to the foot of the dark staircase. I even fancy that, on parting, I hear a kiss exchanged. In Japan this is of no consequence, that I know; it is very usual, and quite admissible ; no matter where one goes, in houses one enters for the first time, one is quite at liberty to kiss any mousmé who may be present, without any notice

being taken of it. But with regard to Chrysanthème, Yves is in a delicate position, and he
ought to understand it better. I begin to feel
uneasy about the hours they have so often spent
together alone; and I make up my mind, that
this very day I will not play the spy upon them,
but speak frankly to Yves, and make a clear
breast of it.

All at once from below, *clac ! clac !* two dry
hands clapped together; it is Madame Prune's
warning to the Great Spirit. And immediately
after her prayer breaks forth, soars upwards in a
shrill nasal falsetto, like a morning alarum when
the hour for waking has come, the mechanical
noise of a spring let go and running down.

"*The richest woman in the world. Cleansed
from all my sins, O Ama-Térace-Omi-Kami, in
the river of Kamo.*"

And this extraordinary bleating, scarcely
human, scatters and changes my ideas, which
were very nearly clear at the moment I awoke.

XLIX.

THERE is a rumour of departure in the air. Since yesterday there has been vague talk of our being sent to China, to the gulf of Pekin ; one of those rumours which spread, no one knows how, from one end of the ship to the other, two or three days before the official orders arrive, and which generally turn out tolerably correct. What will the last act of my little Japanese comedy be like ? the dénouement, the separation ? Will there be any touch of sadness on the part of my mousmé, or on my own, just a tightening of the heart-strings at the moment of our final farewell ? At this moment I can imagine nothing of the sort. And then the adieux of Yves and Chrysanthème, what will they be ? This question preoccupies me more than all.

There is nothing very precise as yet, but it is certain that one way or another, our stay in Japan is coming to an end. It is this perhaps which disposes me this evening, to throw a more friendly glance on my surroundings. It is about six o'clock, after a day spent on duty, when I reach Diou-djen-dji. The evening sun, low in the sky, on the point of setting, pours into my room, and floods it with rays of red gold, lighting up the Buddhas and the great sheaves of quaintly arranged flowers in the antique vases. Here are assembled five or six little dolls, my neighbours, amusing themselves by dancing to the sound of Chrysanthème's guitar. And this evening I experience a real charm in feeling that this dwelling and the woman who leads the dance, are mine. On the whole I have perhaps been unjust to this country ; it seems to me that my eyes are at last opened to see it in its true light, that all my senses are undergoing a strange and abrupt transition ; I suddenly have a better perception and appreciation of all the infinity of dainty trifles amongst which I live ; of the fragile and studied grace of their forms, the oddity of their drawings, the refined choice of their colours.

I stretch myself upon the white mats; Chrysanthème, always eagerly attentive, brings me my pillow of serpent's skin; and the smiling mousmés, with the interrupted rhythm of a while ago still running in their heads, move round me with measured steps.

Their irreproachable socks with the separate great toes, make no noise; nothing is heard, as they glide by, but a froufrou of silken stuffs. I find them all pleasant to look upon; their dollish air has the gift of pleasing me now, and I fancy I have discovered what it is that gives it to them: it is not only their round inexpressive faces with eyebrows far removed from the eyelids, but the excessive amplitude of their dress. With those huge sleeves, it might be supposed they have neither back nor shoulders; their delicate figures are lost in these wide robes, which float around what might be little marionnettes without bodies at all, and which would slip to the ground of themselves were they not kept together mid-way, about where a waist should be, by the wide silken sashes,—a very different comprehension of the art of dressing to ours, which endeavours as much as possible to bring into relief the curves, real or false, of the figure.

And then, how much I admire the flowers arranged by Chrysanthème in our vases, with her Japanese taste : lotus flowers, great  sacred flowers of a tender, veined rose-colour, the milky rose-colour seen on porcelain; they resemble, when in full bloom, great water-lilies, and when only in bud, might be taken for long pale tulips. Their soft but rather cloying scent is added to that other indefinable odour of mousmés, of yellow race, of Japan, which is always and everywhere in the air. The late flowers of September, at this season very rare and expensive, grow on longer stems than the summer blooms; Chrysanthème has left them their immense aquatic leaves of a melancholy seaweed-green, and mingled with them tall slight rushes. I look at them, and recall with some irony those great round bunches in the shape of cauliflowers, which our florists sell in France, wrapt in their white lace-paper.

Still no letters from Europe, from any one. How things change, become effaced and forgotten. Here I am accommodating myself to this finical Japan and dwindling down to its

affected mannerism ; I feel that my thoughts
run in smaller grooves, my tastes incline
to smaller things,—things which suggest
nothing greater than a smile. I am becoming
used to tiny and ingenious furniture, to doll-
like desks, to miniature bowls with which to
play at dinner, to the immaculate monotony of
the mats, to the finely finished simplicity of
the white woodwork. I am even losing my
Western prejudices ; all my preconceived ideas
are this evening evaporating and vanishing ;
crossing the garden I have courteously saluted
M. Sucre, who was watering his dwarf shrubs
and his deformed flowers ; and Madame Prune
appears to me a highly respectable old lady,
in whose past there is nothing to criticise.

We shall take no walk to-night ; my only wish
is to remain stretched out where I am, listening
to the music of my mousmé's *chamécen.*

Till now, I have always used the word *guitar*,
to avoid exotic terms, for the abuse of which I
have been so reproached. But neither the
word *guitar* nor *mandolin* suffices to designate
this slender instrument with its long neck, the
high notes of which are shriller than the voice
of the grasshopper ; henceforth, I will write
chamécen.

I will also call my mousmé *Kikou, Kikou-San ,*

this name suits her better than Chrysanthème,
which though translating the sense exactly,
does not preserve the strange-sounding euphony
of the original.

I therefore say to Kikou, my wife :

" Play, play on for me ; I shall remain here
all the evening and listen to you."

Astonished to find me in so amiable a mood,
she requires pressing a little, and with almost a
bitter curve of triumph and disdain about her
lips, she seats herself in the attitude of an idol,
raises her long, dark-coloured sleeves, and
begins. The first hesitating notes are murmured faintly and mingle with the music of the
insects humming outside, in the quiet air of the
warm and golden twilight. First she plays
slowly, a confused medley of fragments which
she does not seem to remember perfectly, of
which one waits for the finish and waits in
vain ; while the other girls giggle, inattentive,
and regretful of their interrupted dance. She
herself is absent, sulky, as though she were per-
forming a duty only.

Then by degrees, little by little, it becomes
more animated, and the mousmés begin to
listen. Now, tremblingly it grows into a
feverish rapidity, and her gaze has no longer
the vacant stare of a doll. Then the music

changes again ; in it there is the sighing of the wind, the hideous laughter of ghouls ; tears, heartrending plaints, and her dilated pupils seem to be directed inwardly in settled gaze on some indescribable *Japanesery* within her own soul.

I listen, lying there with eyes half shut, looking out between my drooping eyelids which are gradually lowering, in involuntary heaviness, upon the enormous red sun dying away over Nagasaki. I have a somewhat melancholy feeling that my past life and all other places in the world are receding from my view and fading away. At this moment of nightfall I feel almost at home in this corner of Japan, amidst the gardens of this suburb ; I have never had such an impression before.

L.

SEVEN o'clock in the evening. We shall not go down into the town to-day; but, like good Japanese citizens, remain in our lofty suburb.

In undress uniform we shall go, Yves and I, in a neighbourly way, as far as the fencing gallery, which is only two steps off, just above our villa, and almost abutting on our fresh and scented garden.

The gallery is closed already and a little mousko seated at the door, explains with many low bows that we come too late, all the amateurs are gone; we must come again to-morrow.

The evening is so mild and so fine, that we

remain out of doors, following without any definite purpose the pathway which rises ever higher and higher, and loses itself at length in the solitary regions of the mountain among the upper peaks.

For an hour at least we wander on,—an unintended walk,—and finally find ourselves at a great height commanding an endless perspective lighted by the last gleams of daylight ; we are in a desolate and mournful spot, in the midst of the little Buddhist cemeteries, which are scattered over the country in every direction.

We meet a few belated labourers, who are returning from the fields with bundles of tea upon their shoulders. These peasants have a half savage air, half naked too, or clothed only in long robes of blue cotton ; as they pass, they salute us with humble bows.

No trees in this elevated region. Fields of tea alternate with tombs : old granite statues which represent Buddha in his lotus, or else old monumental stones on which gleam remains of inscriptions in golden letters. Rocks, brushwood, uncultivated spaces, surround us on all sides.

There are no more passers-by, and the light is failing. We will halt for a moment, and then it will be time to turn our steps downwards.

But, close to the spot where we stand, a box.

in white wood provided with handles, a sort of sedan-chair, rests on the freshly disturbed earth, with its lotus of silvered paper, and the little incense-sticks burning yet, by its side; clearly someone has been buried here this very evening.

I cannot picture this personage to myself; the Japanese are so grotesque in life, that it is almost impossible to imagine them in the calm majesty of death. Nevertheless, let us move further on, we might disturb him; he is too recently dead, his presence unnerves us We will go and seat ourselves on one of these other tombs, so unutterably ancient that there can no longer be anything within it but dust. And there, seated yet in the dying sunlight, while the valleys and plains of the earth below are already lost in shadow, we will talk together.

I wish to speak to Yves about Chrysanthème; it is indeed somewhat in view of this that I have persuaded him to sit down; but how to set about it without hurting his feelings, and without making myself ridiculous, I hardly know. However, the pure air playing round me up here, and the magnificent landscape spread beneath my feet, impart a certain serenity to my thoughts which makes me feel a contemptuous pity, both for my suspicions and the cause of them.

We speak, first of all, of the order for departure which may arrive at any moment, for China or for France. Soon we shall have to leave this easy and almost amusing life, this Japanese suburb where chance has installed us, and our little house buried among flowers. Yves perhaps will regret all this more than I shall, I know that well enough; for it is the first time that any such interlude has broken the rude monotony of his hard-worked career. Formerly, when in an inferior rank, he was scarcely more often on shore, in foreign countries, than the sea-gulls themselves ; whilst I

have, from the very beginning, been spoilt by residence in all sorts of charming spots, infinitely superior to this, in all sorts of countries, and the remembrance pleasurably haunts me still.

In order to discover how the land lies, I risk the remark :

"You will perhaps be more sorry to leave this little Chrysanthème than I am?"

Silence reigns between us.

After which I pursue, and, burning my ships, I add :

"You know, after all, if you have such a fancy for her, I haven't really married her; one can't really consider her my wife."

In great surprise he looks in my face :

"Not your wife, you say ? But, by Jove, though, that's just it ; she is your wife."

There is no need of many words at any time between us two ; I know exactly now, by his tone, by his great good-humoured smile, how the case stands ; I understand all that lies in the little phrase : "That's just it, she is your wife." If she were not, well then he could not answer for what might happen,—notwithstanding any remorse he might have in the depths of his heart, since he is no longer a bachelor and free as air, as in former days. But he considers her my wife, and she is sacred. I have the fullest faith in his word, and I experience a positive relief, a real joy, at finding my staunch Yves of bygone days. How could I have so succumbed to the demeaning influence of my surroundings as to suspect him even, and invent for myself such a mean, petty anxiety ?

We will never even mention that doll again.

We remain up there very late, talking of other things, gazing the while at the immense depths below our feet, at the valleys and mountains as they become one by one indistinct and lost in the deepening darkness. Placed as we are at an enormous height, in the wide free atmosphere, we seem already to have quitted this miniature country, already to be freed from the impression of littleness which it has given us, and from the little links by which it was beginning to bind us to itself.

Seen from such heights as these, all the countries of the globe bear a strong resemblance to each other; they lose the imprint made upon them by man, and by races; by all the atoms swarming on the surface.

As of old, in the Breton marshes, in the woods of Toulven, or at sea in the night-watches, we talk of all those things to which thoughts naturally revert in darkness; of ghosts, of spirits, of eternity, of the great here-after, of chaos—and we entirely forget little Chrysanthème!

When we arrive at Diou-djen-dji in the starry night, it is the music of her *chamécen*, heard from afar, which recalls to us her existence; she is studying some vocal duet with Mdlle. Oyouki, her pupil.

I feel myself in very good humour this evening, and, relieved from my absurd suspicions about my poor Yves, am quite disposed to enjoy without reserve my last days in Japan, and derive therefrom all the amusement possible.

Let us then stretch ourselves out on the dazzling white mats, and listen to the singular duet sung by these two mousmés : a strange musical medley, slow and mournful, beginning with two or three high notes, and descending at each couplet, in almost an imperceptible manner, into actual solemnity. The song keeps its dragging slowness ; but the accompaniment becoming more and more accentuated, is like the impetuous sound of a far-off hurricane. At the end, when these girlish voices, generally so soft, give out their hoarse and guttural notes, Chrysanthème's hands fly wildly and convulsively over the quivering strings. Both of them lower their heads, pout their under-lips in the effort of bringing out these astonishingly deep notes. And at these moments, their little narrow eyes open and seem to reveal an unexpected something, almost a soul, under these trappings of marionnettes.

But it is a soul which more than ever appears to me of a different species to my own ; I feel my thoughts to be as far removed from theirs, as from the flitting conceptions of a bird, or the dreams of a monkey; I feel there is betwixt

them and myself a great gulf, mysterious and awful.

Other sounds of music, wafted to us from the distance outside, interrupt for a moment that of our mousmés. From the depths below, down

in Nagasaki, arises a sudden noise of gongs and
guitars ; we rush to the balcony of the verandah
to hear it better.

It is a *matsouri*, a fête, a procession passing
through the quarter which is not so virtuous
as our own, so our mousmés tell us, with a
disdainful toss of the head. Nevertheless, from
the heights on which we dwell, seen thus in a
bird's-eye view, by the uncertain light of the
stars, this district has a singularly chaste air,
and the concert going on therein, purified in its
ascent from the depths of the abyss to our lofty
altitudes, reaches us confusedly, a smothered,
enchanted, enchanting sound.

Then it diminishes, and dies away into silence.

The two little friends return to their seats
on the mats, and once more take up their
melancholy duet. An orchestra, discreetly sub-
dued but innumerable, of crickets and cicalas,
accompanies them in an unceasing tremolo,—
the immense far-reaching tremolo, which, gentle
and eternal, never ceases on Japanese land.

LI.

DURING the hour of siesta, the abrupt order arrives to start to-morrow for China, for Tche-fou (a horrid place in the gulf of Pekin). It is Yves who comes to wake me in my cabin to bring me the news.

"I must positively get leave to go on shore this evening," he says, while I endeavour to shake myself awake, "if it is only to help you to dismantle and pack up there."

He gazes through my port-hole, raising his

glance towards the green summits, in the direction of Diou-djen-dji and our echoing old cottage,
hidden from us by a turn of the mountain.

It is very nice of him to wish to help me in
my packing; but I think he also counts upon
saying farewell to his little Japanese friends up
there, and I really cannot find fault with that.

He gets through his work, and does in fact
get leave without help from me, to go on shore
at five o'clock, after drill and manœuvres.

As for myself, I start off at once, in a hired
sampan.   In the vast flood of midday sunshine,
to the quivering noise of the cicalas, I mount
up to Diou-djen-dji.

The paths are solitary, the plants drooping in
the heat.   Here, however, is Madame Jonquille,
taking the air, in the bright sunshine of the
grasshoppers, sheltering her dainty figure and
her charming face under an immense paper
parasol, a huge circle, closely ribbed and fan-
tastically striped.

She recognizes me from afar, and laughing as
usual, runs to meet me.

I announce our departure, and a tearful pout

suddenly contracts her childish face. After all, does this news grieve her? Is she going to shed tears over it? No! it turns to a fit of laughter, a little nervous perhaps, but unexpected and disconcerting,—dry and clear, pealing through the silence and warmth of the narrow paths, like a cascade of little mock pearls.

Ah, there indeed is a marriage tie which will be broken without much pain! But she fills me with impatience, poor empty-headed linnet, with her laughter, and I turn my back upon her to continue my journey.

Up above, Chrysanthème sleeps, stretched out on the floor; the house is wide open, and the soft mountain breeze rustles gently through it.

That same evening we had intended to give a tea-party, and by my orders flowers had already been placed in every nook and corner of the house. There were lotus in our vases, beautiful rose-coloured lotus, the last of the season, I verily believe. They must have been ordered from a special gardener, out yonder near the Great Temple, and they will cost me dear.

With a few gentle taps of a fan I awake my surprised mousmé ; and, curious to catch her first impressions, I announce my departure. She starts up, rubs her eyelids with the back of her little hands, looks at me, and hangs her head : something like an expression of sadness passes in her eyes.

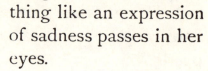

This little sinking at the heart is for Yves, no doubt.

The news spreads through the house.

Mdlle. Oyouki dashes upstairs, with half a tear in each of her babyish eyes ; kisses me with her full red lips, which always leave a wet ring on my cheek ; then quickly draws from her wide sleeve a square of tissue-paper, wipes away her stealthy tears, blows her little nose, rolls the bit of paper in a ball, and throws it into the street on the parasol of a passer-by.

Then Madame Prune makes her appearance ; in an agitated and discomposed manner she successively adopts every attitude expressive of utter dismay. What on earth is the matter with the old lady, and why will she keep getting

Ross,

closer and closer to me, till she is almost in my way?

It is wonderful all I still have to do this last day, and the endless drives I have to make to the old curiosity shops, to my tradespeople, and to the packers.

Nevertheless before my rooms are dismantled, I intend making a sketch of them, as I did formerly at Stamboul. It really seems to me as if all I do here is a bitter parody of all I did over there.

This time, however, it is not that I care for this dwelling ; it is only because it is pretty and uncommon, and the sketch will be an interesting souvenir.

I fetch, therefore, a leaf out of my album, and begin at once, seated on the floor and leaning on my desk, ornamented with grasshoppers in relief, while behind me, very, very close to me, the three women follow the movements of my pencil with an astonished attention. Japanese art being entirely conventional, they have never before seen anyone draw from nature, and my style delights them. I may not perhaps possess the steady and nimble touch of M. Sucre, as he groups his charming storks, but I am master of a few notions of perspective which are wanting in him ; and I have been taught to draw things as I see them, without giving them ingeniously distorted and grimacing attitudes ; and the three Japanese are amazed at the air of *reality* thrown in my sketch.

With little shrieks of admiration, they point
out to each other the different things, as little
by little their shape and form are outlined in
black on my paper.   Chrysanthème gazes at
me with a new kind of interest : "*Anata itchi-*
ban!" she says (literally "Thou first!" meaning : "You are really quite a swell!")

Mdlle. Oyouki is carried away by her admiration and exclaims in a burst of enthusiasm :

"*Anata bakari!*" ("Thou alone!" that is to
say : "There is no one like you in the world, all
the rest are mere rubbish!")

Madame Prune says nothing, but I can see
that she does not think the less ; her languishing
attitudes, her hand that at each moment gently
touches mine, confirm the suspicions that her
look of dismay a few moments ago awoke
within me : evidently my physical charms speak
to her imagination, which in spite of years has
remained full of romance!   I shall leave with
the regret of having understood her too late!!

If the ladies are satisfied with my sketch, I
am far from being so.   I have put everything
in its place most exactly, but as a whole, it has
an ordinary, indifferent, French look which does
not suit.   The sentiment is not given, and I
almost wonder whether I should not have done

better in falsifying the perspective,—Japanese style—and exaggerating to the very utmost the already abnormal outlines of what I see before me. And then the pictured dwelling lacks the fragile look and its sonority, that reminds one of a dry violin. In the pencilled delineation of the woodwork, the minute delicacy

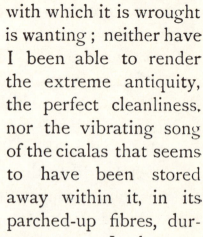

with which it is wrought is wanting ; neither have I been able to render the extreme antiquity, the perfect cleanliness, nor the vibrating song of the cicalas that seems to have been stored away within it, in its parched-up fibres, during some hundreds of summers. It does not either convey the impression this place gives of being in a far-off suburb, perched aloft among trees, above the drollest of towns. No, all this cannot be drawn, cannot be expressed, but remains undemonstrable, undefinable.

Having sent out our invitations, we shall in spite of everything, give our tea-party this evening,—a parting tea, therefore, in which we will display as much pomp as possible.

It is, moreover, rather my custom to wind up my exotic existences with a fête ; in other countries I have done the same.

Besides our usual set, we shall have my mother-in-law, my relatives, and all the mousmés of the neighbourhood.   But, by an extra Japanese refinement, we shall not admit a single European friend,—not even the *amazingly tall*

one.   Yves alone shall be admitted, and even
he shall be hidden away in a corner behind
some flowers and works of art.

In the last glimmer of twilight, by the first
twinkling star, the ladies, with many charming
curtseys, make their appearance.   Our house is
soon full of the little crouching women, with
their tiny slit eyes vaguely smiling ; their beautifully dressed hair shining like polished ebony ;
their fragile bodies lost in the many folds of the
exaggerated wide garments, that gape as if ready
to drop from their little tapering backs and
reveal the exquisite napes of their little necks.

Chrysanthème, with somewhat a melancholy air ; my mother-in-law Renoncule, with
many affected graces, busy themselves in the
midst of the different groups, where ere long
the miniature pipes are lighted.   Soon there
arises a murmuring sound of discreet laughter,
expressing nothing, but having a pretty exotic
ring about it, and then begins a harmony of *pan !*
pan ! pan ! sharp, rapid taps against the edges
of the finely lacquered smoking-boxes.   Pickled
and spiced fruits are handed round on trays of
quaint and varied shapes.   Then transparent
china tea-cups, no larger than half an egg-shell,
make their appearance, and the ladies are

offered a few drops of sugarless tea, poured out of toy kettles, or a sip of *saki*—(a spirit made from rice which it is the custom to serve hot, in elegantly shaped vases, long-necked like a heron's throat).

Several mousmés execute, one after the other, improvisations on the *chamécen*. Others sing in sharp high voices hopping about continually, like cicalas in delirium.

Madame Prune, no longer able to make a mystery of the long-pent up feelings that agitate her, pays me the most marked and tender attentions, and begs my acceptance of a quantity of little souvenirs : an image, a little vase, a little porcelain goddess of the Moon in Satsuma ware, a marvellously grotesque ivory figure ;—I tremblingly follow her into the dark corners whither she calls me to give me these presents in a *tête-à-tête*.

At about nine o'clock, with a silken rustling, arrive the three guéchas in vogue in Nagasaki : Mdlles. Pureté, Orange, and Printemps, whom I have hired at four dollars a head,—an enormous price in this country.

These three guéchas are indeed the very same little creatures I heard singing on the rainy day of my arrival, through the thin panelling of the

Garden of Flowers. But as I have now become thoroughly *Japanised,* to-day they appear to me more diminutive, less outlandish, and in no way mysterious. I treat them rather as dancers that I have hired, and the idea that I had ever thought of marrying one of them now makes me shrug my shoulders,— as it formerly did M. Kangourou.

The excessive heat caused by the respiration of the mousmés and the burning lamps, brings out the perfume of the lotus, which fills the heavy-laden atmosphere; and the scent of the camelia-oil the ladies use in profusion to make their hair glisten, is also strong in the room.

Mdlle. Orange, the youngest guécha, tiny and dainty, her lips outlined with gilt paint, executes some delightful steps, donning the most extraordinary wigs and masks in wood or cardboard. She has masks imitating old noble ladies which are valuable works of art, signed by well-known artists. She has also magnificent long robes, fashioned in the old style, and trains trimmed at the bottom with thick pads, in order to give to the movements of the costume something rigid and unnatural which, however, is becoming.

Now the soft balmy breezes blow through the room, from one verandah to the other, making the flames of the lamps flicker. They scatter the lotus flowers faded by the artificial heat, which, falling in pieces from every vase, sprinkle the guests with their pollen  and large pink petals, looking like bits of broken opal-coloured glass.

The sensational piece, reserved for the end, is a trio on the *chamécen*, long and monotonous, that the guéchas perform as a rapid *pizzicato* on the highest strings, very sharply struck. It sounds like the very quintescence, the paraphrase, the exasperation if I may so call it, of the eternal buzz of insects, which issues from the trees, old roofs, old walls, from everything in fact, and which is the ground-work of ll Japanese sounds.

Half-past ten ! The programme has been carried out, and the reception is over. A last general *pan! pan! pan!* the little pipes are stowed away into their chased sheaths, tied p in the sashes, and the mousmés rise to depart.

They light, at the end of short sticks, a quantity of red, grey or blue lanterns, and after a series of endless bows and curtseys, the guests disperse themselves in the darkness of the lanes and trees.

We also go down to the town,—Yves, Chrysanthème, Oyouki, and myself,—in order to conduct my mother-in-law, sisters-in-law, and youthful aunt, Madame Nénufar, to their house.

We want to take one last stroll together in our old familiar pleasure haunts, drink one more iced sherbet at the house of the *Indescribable Butterflies*, buy one more lantern at Madame Très-Propre's, and eat some parting waffles at Madame L'Heure's !

I try to be affected, moved, by this leave-

taking, but without success.   In this Japan, as
with the little men and women who inhabit it,
there is something decidedly wanting ; pleasant
enough as a mere pastime, it begets no feeling
of attachment.

On our return, when I am once more with
Yves and the two mousmés climbing up the
road to Diou-djen-dji, which I shall probably
never see again, a vague feeling of melancholy
pervades my last stroll.

It is, however, but the melancholy inseparable
from all things that are about to end without
possibility of return.

Moreover, this calm and splendid summer is
also drawing to a close for us,—since to-morrow
we shall go forth to meet the autumn, in
Northern China.   I am beginning, alas ! to
count the youthful summers I may still hope
for ; I feel more gloomy each time another
fades away, and flies to rejoin the others already
disappeared in the dark and bottomless abyss,
where all past things lie buried.

At midnight we return home, and my removal
begins ; while on board the *amazingly tall friend*
kindly takes my watch.

It is a nocturnal, rapid, stealthy removal,—

"*dorobo* (thieves) fashion" remarks Yves, who in frequenting the mousmés has picked up a smattering of the Niponese language.

Messrs. the packers have, at my request, sent in the evening several charming little boxes, with compartments and false bottoms, and several paper bags (in the untearable Japanese paper), which close of  themselves and are fastened by strings, also in paper, arranged beforehand in the most ingenious manner,—quite the cleverest and most handy thing of its kind; for little useful trifles these people are unrivalled.

It is a real treat to pack them, and everybody lends a helping hand,—Yves, Chrysanthème, Madame Prune, her daughter, and M. Sucre. By the glimmer of the reception-lamps, which are still burning, everyone wraps, rolls, and ties up expeditiously, for it is already late.

Although Oyouki has a heavy heart, she cannot prevent herself from indulging in a few bursts of childish laughter while she works.

Madame Prune, bathed in tears, no longer restrains her feelings; poor lady, I really very much regret....

Chrysanthème is absentminded and silent.

But what a fearful amount of luggage! Eighteen cases or parcels, containing Buddhas, chimeras, and vases, without mentioning the last lotus that I carry away tied up in a pink cluster.

All this is piled up in the djins' carts, hired at sunset, which are waiting at the door, while their runners lie asleep on the grass.

A starlit and exquisite night. We start off with lighted lanterns, followed by the three sorrowful ladies who accompany us, and by abrupt slopes, dangerous in the darkness, we descend towards the sea.

The djins, stiffening their muscular legs, hold back with all their might the heavily loaded little cars which would run down by themselves if let alone, and that so rapidly, that they would rush into empty space with my most valuable chattels. Chrysanthème walks by my side, and expresses, in a soft and winning manner, her regret that the *wonderfully tall friend* did not offer to replace me for the whole of my night-watch, as that would have allowed me to spend this last night, even till morning, under our roof.

" Listen," she says, " come back to-morrow in the daytime, before getting under way, to bid me good-bye ; I shall only return to my mother in the evening ; you will find me still up there."

And I promise.

They stop at a certain turn, from whence we have a bird's-eye view of the whole roadstead ; the black stagnant waters reflect innumerable distant fires, and the ships—tiny immoveable little objects, which seen from our point of view take the shape of fish, seem also to slumber,— little objects which serve to bear us *elsewhere*, to go far away, and to forget.

The three ladies are going to turn back home, for the night is already far advanced, and lower down, the cosmopolitan quarters near the quays are not safe at this unusual hour.

The moment has therefore come for Yves— who will not land again—to make his last tragic farewells to his friends the little mousmés.

Now I am very curious to see the parting between Yves and Chrysanthème ; I listen with all my ears, I look with all my eyes, it takes place in the simplest and quietest fashion : none of that heartbreaking which will be inevitable be- tween Madame Prune and myself ; I even notice in my mousmé an indifference, an unconcern which puzzles me ; I positively am at a loss to understand what it all means.

And I muse to myself as I continue to descend towards the sea. " Her appearance of sadness was not, therefore, on Yves' account. On whose, then ? " and the phrase runs through my head :

" Come back to-morrow before setting sail, to bid me good-bye ; I shall only return to my mother in the evening ; you will find me still up there."

Japan is indeed most delightful this evening, so fresh and so sweet ; and little Chrysan- thème was very charming just now, as she

silently walked beside me through the darkness
of the lane.

It is about two o'clock when we reach the
Triomphante in a hired sampan, where I have
heaped up all my cases till there is danger of
sinking. The *very tall friend* gives over to me
the watch that I must keep till four o'clock;
and the sailors on duty, but half awake, make a
chain in the darkness, to haul on board all **my**
fragile luggage.

LII.

I HAD planned to sleep late this morning, in order to make up for my lost sleep of last night.

But behold, at eight o'clock, three persons of the most singular appearance, led by M. Kangourou, present themselves with endless bows at the door of my cabin. They are dressed in long robes bedizened with dark patterns; they have the flowing locks, high foreheads and pallid countenances of persons too exclusively devoted to the fine arts; and, perched on the top of their chignons, they wear sailor hats of English shape

stuck jauntily on one side. Under their arms,
they carry portfolios filled with sketches ; in
their hands, boxes of water-colours, pencils, and,
tied together like fasces, a bundle of fine stylets
the sharp points of which glitter ostensibly.

At the first
glance, even in
the bewilder-
ment of wak-
ing, I gather
from their ap-
pearance what
their errand is,
and guessing
with what visi-
tors I have to
deal, I say :—
" Come in,
Messieurs the
tattooers ! "

These are
the specialists
most in renown
in Nagasaki ; I had engaged them two days ago,
not knowing that we were about to leave, and
since they are come I will not turn them away.

My friendly and intimate relations with pri
mitive man, in Oceania and elsewhere, have im-

bued me with a deplorable taste for tattoo work;
and I had wished to carry away on me, as a
curiosity, an ornament, a specimen of the work

of the Japanese tattooers, who have a delicacy
of finish which is unequalled.

From their albums spread out upon my table
I make my choice. There are some remarkably
odd designs amongst them, appropriate to the

different parts of the human body : emblems for the arms and legs, sprays of roses for the shoulders, great grinning faces for the middle of the back. There are even, to suit the taste of their clients who belong to foreign navies, trophies of arms, American and French flags entwined, a "God Save the Queen" amid encircling stars, and figures of women taken from Grévin's sketches in the *Journal Amusant*.

My choice rests upon a singular blue and pink dragon a couple of inches long, which will have a fine effect upon my chest on the side opposite the heart.

Then follows an hour and a half of irritation and positive pain. Stretched out on my bunk and delivered over to the tender mercies of these personages, I stiffen myself and submit to the million imperceptible pricks they inflict. When by chance a little blood flows, confusing the outline by a stream of red, one of the artists hastens to staunch it with his lips, and I make no objections, knowing that this is the Japanese manner, the method used by their doctors for the wounds of both man and beast.

A piece of work as minute and fine as that of an engraver upon stone is slowly executed on my person ; and their lean hands harrow and worry me with automatic precision.

At length it is finished, and the tattooers, falling back with an air of satisfaction to contemplate their work, declare it will be lovely.

I dress myself quickly to go on shore, and take advantage of my last hours in Japan.

The heat is fearful to-day: the powerful September sun falls with a certain melancholy upon the yellowing leaves; it is a day of clear burning heat after an almost chilly morning.

Like yesterday, it is during the drowsy noon that I ascend to my lofty suburb, by deserted pathways filled only with light and silence.

I noiselessly open the door of my dwelling, and enter cautiously on tiptoe, for fear of Madame Prune.

At the foot of the staircase, upon the white mats, by the side of the little clogs and little sandals which are always lying about the vestibule, there is a great array of luggage ready for departure, which I recognise at a glance,—pretty dark-coloured dresses, familiar to my sight, carefully folded and wrapped in blue towels tied at the four corners. I even fancy I feel a little sad when I catch sight of a corner of the famous box of letters and souvenirs peeping out of one of these bundles, in which my portrait by Uyenu now reposes among divers photographs of mousmés. A sort of long-necked mandolin, also ready for departure, lies on the top of the pile in its case of figured silk. It resembles the flitting of some gipsy, or rather it reminds me of an engraving in a book of fables I owned in my childhood: the whole thing is exactly like the slender wardrobe and the long guitar which the Cicala who had sung all the summer, carried upon her back when she knocked at the door of her neighbour the ant.

Poor little gipsy!

I mount the stairs on tiptoe, and stop at the sound of singing that I hear up in my room.

It is undoubtedly Chrysanthème's voice and the song is a cheerful one! This chills me and changes the current of my thoughts. I am almost sorry I have taken the trouble to come.

Mingled with the song is a noise I cannot understand: *dzinn! dzinn!* a clear metallic ring as of coins being flung vigorously on the floor. I am well aware that this vibrating house exaggerates every sound during the silence of night; but all the same, I am puzzled to know what my mousmé can be doing. *Dzinn! dzinn!* is she amusing herself with quoits, or the *jeu du crapaud*, or pitch and toss?

Nothing of the kind ! I fancy I have guessed, and I continue my upward progress still more gently, on all fours, with the precautions of a Red Indian, to give myself for the last time the pleasure of surprising her.

She has not heard me come in. In our great white room, emptied and swept out, where the clear sunshine pours in, and the soft wind, and the yellowed leaves of the garden ; she is sitting all alone, her back turned to the door : she is dressed for walking, ready to go to her mother's, her rose-coloured parasol beside her.

On the floor are spread out all the fine silver dollars which, according to our agreement, I had given her the evening before. With the competent dexterity of an old money-changer she fingers them, turns them over, throws them on the floor, and armed with a little mallet *ad hoc*, rings them vigorously against her ear, singing the while I know not what little pensive bird-like song which I daresay she improvises as she goes along.

Well after all, it is even more completely Japanese than I could possibly have imagined it—this last scene of my married life ! I feel inclined to laugh. How simple I have been, to allow myself to be taken in by the few clever words she whispered yesterday, as she walked beside me, by a tolerably pretty little phrase embellished as it was by the silence of two o'clock

in the morning, and all the wonderful enchantments of night.

Ah! not more for Yves than for me, not more for me than for Yves, has any feeling passed through that little brain, that little heart. When I have

looked at her long enough, I call :—

" Hi! Chrysanthème! "

She turns confused, and reddening even to her ears at having been caught at this work.

She is quite wrong, however, to be so much

troubled, for I am, on the contrary, delighted. The fear that I might be leaving her in some

sadness had almost given me a pang, and I infinitely prefer that this marriage should end as it had begun, in a joke.

"That is a good idea of yours," I say; "a precaution which should always be taken in this country of yours, where so many evil-minded people are clever in forging money. Make haste and get through it before I start, and if any false pieces have found their way into the number, I will willingly replace them."

However, she refuses to continue before me, and I expected as much ; to do so would have been contrary to all her notions of politeness, hereditary and acquired, all her conventionality, all her *Japanesery*. With a disdainful little foot, clothed as usual in exquisite socks with a special hood for the great toe, she pushes away the piles of white dollars and scatters them on the mats.

"We have hired a large covered sampan," she says to change the conversation, "and we are all going together,—Campanule, Jonquille, Touki, all your mousmés—to watch your vessel set sail. Pray sit down and stay a few minutes."

"No, I really cannot stay. I have several things to do in the town, d'you see, and the order was given for every one to be on board by three o'clock in time for muster before starting. Moreover, I would rather escape, as you can imagine, while Madame Prune is still enjoying her siesta ; I should be afraid of being drawn into some corner, or of provoking some heartrending parting scene."

Chrysanthème bows her head and says no more, but seeing that I am really going, rises to escort me

Without speaking, without the slightest noise, she follows me as we descend the staircase and cross the garden full of sunshine, where the dwarf shrubs and the deformed flowers seem, like the rest of the household, plunged in warm somnolence.

At the outer gate I stop for the last adieu : the little sad pout has reappeared, more accentuated than ever on Chrysanthème's face ; it is the right thing, it is correct, and I should feel offended now were it absent.

Well, little mousmé, let us part good friends ; one last kiss even, if you like. I took you to amuse me ; you have not perhaps succeeded very well, but after all you have done what you could : given me your little face, your little curtseys, your little music ; in short, you have been pleasant enough in your Japanese way. And who knows, perchance I may yet think of you sometimes when I recall this glorious summer, these pretty quaint gardens, and the ceaseless concert of the cicalas.

She prostrates herself on the threshold of the

door, her forehead against the ground, and remains in this attitude of superlatively polite salute as long as I am in sight, while I go down the pathway by which I am to disappear for ever.

As the distance between us increases, I turn once or twice to look at her again; but it is a mere civility, and meant to return as it deserves her grand final salutation.

LIII.

On entering the town, at the turn of the
principal street, I have the good luck to meet
No. 415, my poor relation.   I was just at that
moment in want of a speedy djin, and I at once
get into his vehicle ; besides, it will be an allevia-
tion to my feelings, in this hour of departure, to
take my last drive in company with a member
of my family.

Unaccustomed as I was to be out of doors
during the hours of siesta, I had never yet seen
the streets of the town thus overwhelmed by
the sunshine, thus deserted in the silence and
solitary brilliancy peculiar to all hot countries.

In front of all the shops hang white shades, adorned here and there with slight designs in black, in the quaintness of which lurks I know not what,—something mysterious : dragons, emblems, symbolical figures. The sky is too glaring; the light crude, implacable; never has this old town of Nagasaki appeared to me so old, so worm-eaten, so bald, notwithstanding all its veneer of new papers and gaudy paintings. These little wooden houses, of such marvellous cleanly whiteness inside, are black outside, time-worn, disjointed and *grimacing*. When one looks closely, this grimace is to be found everywhere : in the hideous masks laughing in the shop fronts of the innumerable curio-shops ; in the grotesque figures, the playthings, the idols, cruel, suspicious, mad ;—it is even found in the buildings : in the friezes of the religious porticos, in the roofs of the thousand pagodas, of which the angles and cable-ends writhe and twist like the yet dangerous remains of ancient and malignant beasts.

And the disturbing intensity of expression reigning over inanimate nature, contrasts with the almost absolute blank of the human countenance, with the smiling foolishness of the simple little folk who meet one's gaze, as they patiently carry on their minute trades in the gloom of

their tiny open-fronted houses. Workmen
squatted on their heels, carving with their imperceptible tools, the droll or odiously obscene
ivory ornaments, marvellous cabinet curiosities
which have made Japan so famous with the
European amateurs who have never seen it.
Unconscious artists tracing with steady hand
on a background of lacquer or of porcelain
traditional designs learnt by heart, or trans-
mitted to their brains by a process of heredity
through thousands of years ; automatic painters,
whose storks are similar to those of M. Sucre,
with the inevitable little rocks, or little butterflies eternally the same. The least of these
illuminators, with his insignificant eyeless face,
possesses at his fingers' ends the maximum of
dexterity in this art of decoration, light and
wittily incongruous, which threatens to invade us
in France, in this epoch of imitative decadence,
and which has become the great resource of
our manufacturers of cheap "*objects of art.*"

Is it because I am about to leave this country,
because I have no longer any link to bind me
to it, any resting-place on its soil, and that my
spirit is ready on the wing ? I know not, but
seems to me I have never as clearly seen and
comprehended it as to-day. And more even
than ever, do I find it little, aged, with worn-

out blood and worn-out sap ; I feel more fully
its antediluvian antiquity, its centuries of mum-
mification, which will soon degenerate into
hopeless and grotesque buffoonery, as it comes
into contact with Western novelties.

It is getting late ; little by little, the siestas
 are everywhere coming
to an end ; the queer
little streets brighten
up and begin to swarm
in the sunshine with
many-coloured parasols.
Now begins the proces-
sion of uglinesses of the
most impossible descrip-
tion,—a procession of
long-robed, grotesque figures capped with pot-
hats or sailors' head-gear. Business transactions
begin again, and the struggle for existence,
close and bitter here as in one of our own artisan
quarters, but meaner and smaller.

At the moment of my departure, I can only
find within myself a smile of careless mockery
for the swarming crowd of this Liliputian curt-
seying people,—laborious, industrious, greedy
of gain, tainted with a constitutional affectation, hereditary insignificance, and incurable
monkeyishness.

Poor cousin 415, how right I was to have

held him in good esteem ; he is by far the best
and most disinterested of my Japanese family.
When all my commissions are finished, he puts
up his little vehicle under a tree, and much
touched by my departure, insists upon escorting

me on board the *Triomphante*, to watch over
my final purchases in the sampan which conveys me to the ship, and to see them himself
safely into my cabin.

His, indeed, is the only hand I clasp with a
really friendly feeling, without a suppressed
smile, on quitting this Japan.

No doubt, in this country as in many others, there is more honest friendship and less ugliness among the simple beings devoted to purely physical work.

At five o'clock in the afternoon we set sail.

Along the line of the shore are two or three sampans ; in them the mousmés, shut up in the narrow cabins, peep at us through the tiny windows, half hiding their faces on account of the sailors ; these are our wives, who have wished, out of politeness, to look upon us once more.

There are other sampans as well, in which other Japanese women are also watching our departure. These stand upright, under great parasols decorated with big black letters and daubed over with clouds of varied and startling colours.

LIV.

W<small>E</small> move slowly out of the great green bay. The groups of women become lost in the distance. The country of round and thousand-ribbed umbrellas fades gradually from our sight.

Now the great sea opens before us, immense, colourless, solitary ; a solemn repose after so much that was too ingenious and too small.

The wooded mountains, the charming capes
disappear.   And Japan remains faithful to itself
in its last picturesque rocks, its quaint islands
on which the trees tastefully arrange themselves in groups—studied perhaps, but charmingly pretty.

LV.

IN my cabin, one evening, in the midst of
the Yellow Sea, my eyes chance to fall upon
the lotus brought from Diou-djen-dji;—they had
lasted for two or three days; but now they are
faded, and pitifully strew my carpet with their
pale pink petals.

I, who have carefully preserved so many
faded flowers, fallen, alas! into dust, stolen here
and there, at moments of parting in different
parts of the world; I who have kept so many,

that the collection is now almost a herbarium ridiculous and incoherent — I try hard, but without success, to get up a sentiment for these lotus—and yet they are the last living souvenirs of my summer at Nagasaki.

I pick them up, however, with a certain amount of consideration, and I open my port-hole.

From the grey misty sky a livid light falls upon the waters ; a wan and gloomy kind of twilight creeps down, yellowish upon this Yellow Sea. We feel that we are moving northwards, that autumn is approaching.

I throw the poor lotus into the boundless waste of waters, making them my best excuses for giving to them, natives of Japan, a grave so solemn and so vast.

LVI.

O Ama-Térace-Omi-Kami, wash me clean from this little marriage of mine, in the waters of the river of Kamo.

MORE ABOUT KPI BOOKS

If you would like further information about books available from KPI please write to

> The Marketing Department
> KPI Limited
> Routledge & Kegan Paul Plc
> 14 Leicester Square
> London WC2H 7PH

In the USA write to

> The Marketing Department
> KPI Limited
> Routledge & Kegan Paul
> 9 Park Street
> Boston
> Mass 02108

In Australia write to

> The Marketing Department
> KPI Limited
> Routledge & Kegan Paul
> c/o Methuen Law Book Company
> 44 Waterloo Road
> North Ryde, NSW 2113
> Australia

KPI